THE JOURNEY OF FORGIVENESS

A Workbook for Healing, Freedom and Transformation

By Katherine Bluma

THE JOURNEY OF FORGIVENESS

A Workbook for Healing, Freedom and Transformation

By Katherine Bluma

The Journey of Forgiveness
A Workbook for Healing, Freedom and Transformation

Author: Katherine Bluma.
Published by: Forgiveness Freedom Fighter
Front and Back Cover by: Jewel Johnson
Editing by: Jessica Cernetic and Jewel Johnson
Copyright © 2024 by Forgiveness Freedom Fighter. All rights reserved.

The concepts, activities, worksheets, and all related materials contained in this publication are the intellectual property of Katherine Bluma and Forgiveness Freedom Fighter and are protected by copyright and other intellectual property laws.

No part of this publication may be reproduced, distributed, or transmitted in any form or by any means, including photocopying, recording, or any information storage and retrieval system, without the prior written permission of Katherine Bluma and Forgiveness Freedom Fighter.

Modification, adaptation, or use of the materials for commercial purposes is strictly prohibited without express written consent from Katherine Bluma and Forgiveness Freedom Fighter.

These materials are intended for personal, educational, and non-commercial use only. If you wish to share these materials, please do so by directing others to purchase their own copies or to obtain permission for specific use.

For permission requests or inquiries regarding licensing, please submit a form at
www.ForgivenessFreedomFighter.com/ContactUs

Copyright © 1960, 1971, 1977, 1995, 2020 by The Lockman Foundation.
Scripture quotations taken from the (NASB®) New American Standard Bible®
Used by permission. All rights reserved. lockman.org"

TABLE OF CONTENTS

Acknowledgements		1
Section 1:	A Warrior's Beginning	3
Section 2:	The Role of Emotions in Forgiveness	18
Section 3:	Preparation of the Heart and Mind	32
Section 4:	Starting the Forgiveness Journey	44
Section 5:	Navigating Grief in Forgiveness	60
Section 6:	Embracing God's Truth	70
Section 7:	The Labels That Define Us	78
Section 8:	The Path to Self Forgiveness	92
Section 9:	Walking in Long Suffering	106
Section 10:	The Forgiveness Jellyfish	114
Section 11:	Uncovering Hidden Hurt	130
Section 12:	The Gifts of Forgiveness	142
Section 13:	The Power of Apology	152
Section 14:	Steps Toward Reconciliation	166
Section 15:	Learning to Live Blamelessly	172
Section 16:	Caring for Body and Soul	182
Bonus Materials		234
Leveraging Our Team		270

ACKNOWLEDGEMENTS

All of my love and appreciation go to The Lord Jesus the Christ, The One who walked beside me, guiding me through this process—sometimes gently, sometimes firmly—over the past 12 years: You refined both me and this work. Recently, I felt Your stirring in my soul, urging me to commit this work to paper. Thank You for equipping Your church to let go of past hurts and embrace the life of freedom that only You can provide.

My deepest gratitude goes to my husband, Joe Dean, and my business partner, Jewel Johnson. Your support and encouragement made this work possible. Words cannot adequately express my thanks; I am grateful every day.

I must acknowledge Aurora, who dragged me—kicking in defiance—into a retreat where my journey into forgiveness work began. The Lord knew the good work that would start that weekend.

To all the other countless fellow disciples and warriors for our Savior: your stories became the inspiration to persevere.

Thank you.

SECTION 1

A Warrior's Beginning

In this opening section, we set the foundation for the journey ahead, exploring the multifaceted definition of a warrior in faith, understanding the significance of addressing God as "Abba," and explaining why we use the NASB Bible throughout the workbook.

You'll also discover the powerful symbolism of the rainbow and butterfly, representing God's promises and the transformative nature of forgiveness.

We begin by unpacking what forgiveness truly is—and what it is not—laying the groundwork for your path toward healing and freedom.

WELCOME TO A TRANSFORMATIVE JOURNEY OF HEALING AND SELF-DISCOVERY.

This workbook is more than a collection of pages; it's a warrior's guide for your personal quest, leading you from the shadows of hurt and betrayal into the radiant light of understanding, peace, and forgiveness.

Like a rainbow emerging after a storm, this journey will take you through the full spectrum of emotions. It will challenge you to face the dark clouds of your past, but also promise the vibrant colors of hope and renewal on the other side.

As you embark on this path, consider yourself a spiritual warrior, armed with the tools of introspection and the strength of forgiveness. This workbook will be your shield and sword, helping you battle the inner demons of resentment and pain, and ultimately guiding you to victory over the burdens that have held you back.

Your journey starts here, brave warrior. Are you ready to step into the arena of self- discovery and emerge transformed?

My own path began in a place of profound pain, where hope seemed a distant dream. Amidst the turmoil of betrayal and abuse, I found myself at a crossroads. It was in my darkest moments, contemplating escape through any means, that I discovered the transformative power of forgiveness—a power that not only healed my heart but rekindled connections I had lost over the years.

This workbook distills that journey, interweaving stories, principles, and exercises that guided me toward healing. Each activity unfolds a step in the forgiveness process, encouraging deep reflection, offering spiritual insights from scripture, and providing practical steps to apply these lessons in your life.

Here, you'll explore the depths of your pain, confront lingering shadows, and learn to release them. You'll discover how to forgive not just others, but yourself, unlocking a new chapter of peace and fulfillment.

Let this be your lantern in the darkness, illuminating the path to healing and freedom. Through these pages, may you find the courage to face your fears, the strength to break free from your chains, and the wisdom to embrace forgiveness.

Embracing truth and reality demands courage, but the rewards—peace, self-love, and potential reconciliation—far outweigh the effort. This marks the beginning of a life free from bitterness, resentment, and unhealthy attachments.

Move through each section at your own pace.

It's an honor to share the principles I've learned over the years, insights gleaned from the Holy Spirit's gentle nudges, Bible study, and the wisdom of fellow believers.

Remember, this is just the starting point. This workbook offers tools to cultivate spiritual growth and a life free from unnecessary burdens. As you progress, may you find the strength and courage to face each step with TRUTH, hope, and determination. Then you can make the commitment to be a person who forgives, you just choose it!

Your Fellow Warrior and Journeyman,

Kat

THE MULTIFACETED DEFINITION OF A WARRIOR

1. Traditional: A person engaged in warfare or a soldier.

2. Spiritual: One who battles in the spiritual realm.

3. Philosophical: Dan Millman describes a warrior as someone who "lives with courage, awareness, and integrity," focusing on mental and moral qualities.

4. Cultural: In ancient cultures like Japan, warriors (e.g., Samurai) followed a strict code of honor, discipline, and loyalty.

5. Psychological: In modern psychology, a "warrior" can refer to someone who overcomes significant adversity, such as trauma survivors or those battling chronic illness.

All these definitions hold truth. Becoming a warrior, in any sense, is possible through faith in Jesus Christ.

This workbook will guide you through processes I've learned from personal experiences, conferences, books, therapy, prayer, and meditation—cornerstones of my Christian journey. You can use this resource repeatedly, apply it to your relationships, and even share it with your pastor or therapist when you need support.

Throughout this journey, you'll discover that the Holy Spirit is your guide and healer. Remember, Jesus Christ, the only One with the authority to forgive sins, has already reached out to you. It's time to receive His gifts: forgiveness, peace, freedom, and an abundance of love for yourself and others. Be compassionate with yourself, this journey exists because of the pain that bestowed upon you.

Now is the time to free yourself from its power.

THE DIFFERENT VERSIONS OF THE BIBLE

The Bible has been translated into many versions, each with its own unique approach to conveying the meaning of the original texts. These translations vary in their methods, with some prioritizing readability and others focusing on capturing the exact wording from the original Hebrew, Aramaic, and Greek. Among the various translations, the New American Standard Bible (NASB) is widely regarded for its commitment to precision and faithfulness to the original manuscripts.

The NASB emphasizes a word-for-word translation, often referred to as "formal equivalence." This approach seeks to stay as close as possible to the wording and structure of the original languages, making it an excellent choice for those desiring an in-depth understanding of the Bible's message. While some translations may adopt a more dynamic or paraphrased approach to improve readability, the NASB preserves the nuances of the original texts, ensuring that key theological concepts and truths are not lost or altered.

The use of the NASB in this book serves an important purpose. Because forgiveness is a deeply spiritual and transformative journey, it is essential that the scriptures referenced are presented with clarity and accuracy. The NASB's focus on linguistic precision ensures that the verses used throughout this book retain their integrity, providing a reliable foundation for the insights and teachings related to healing, reconciliation, and spiritual growth.

While other translations, such as the NIV (New International Version) or the NLT (New Living Translation), may be easier to read for some, the NASB offers a depth and exactness that makes it particularly valuable for study and reflection. By using the NASB throughout this book, the goal is to provide readers with a clear, faithful representation of God's Word that supports them in their pursuit of forgiveness and spiritual renewal.

A SYMBOL OF HIS PROMISE

The rainbow stands as a testament to God's promise. From our earthly perspective, we see only half its arc, but from above, its full circle is revealed. This celestial ring symbolizes how God's love encompasses His children completely.

Just as the unseen portion of the rainbow exists beyond our view, God's work often unfolds beyond our immediate perception. Yet, like the rainbow's hidden half, His love and mercy encircle us always, even when we cannot directly witness their presence.

In moments of doubt, remember this...

The rainbow's partial appearance does not diminish its wholeness. Similarly, our limited view of God's plan does not lessen its perfection or His constant care for us.

A SYMBOL OF TRANSFORMATION

In this book, the butterfly serves as a symbol of transformation, renewal, and new beginnings—echoing the spiritual journey of forgiveness, healing, and growth.

Just as the butterfly undergoes a profound change from a caterpillar to a winged creature, we too are invited to experience transformation through God's grace.

The butterfly's journey mirrors the believer's call to leave behind old ways, to be renewed by the Spirit, and to emerge into the fullness of life that God offers.

As you progress through this book, may the butterfly serve as a visual representation of your own transformation—of the beauty and strength that comes from surrendering to God's process of healing and growth.

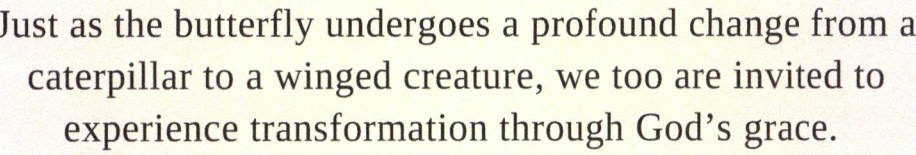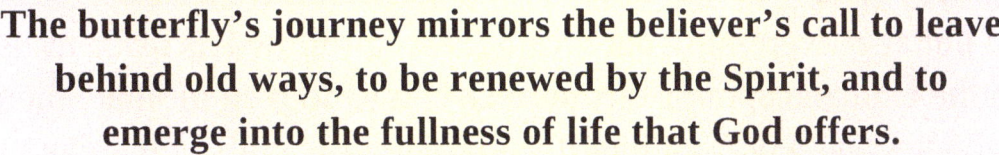

APPROACHING GOD AS ABBA

In this workbook, you will see prayers that address God as "Abba," a term that carries deep meaning and significance.

The word "Abba" is more than just a name; it embodies intimacy, trust, and a willingness to follow God's will. When Jesus taught His disciples to pray, the first word He instructed them to use was "Father." But in His own most intimate moments, like in the Garden of Gethsemane, Jesus addressed God as "Abba, Father"—a phrase that combines both the familiar Greek term for father, "pater," and the Aramaic "Abba," which expresses a heart-level closeness. This name shows us that God is not only the Creator and Ruler of all but also our loving Father, inviting us into an intimate relationship with Him.

"Abba" goes beyond being a term of affection; it's also a word that calls for obedience and discipleship.

When we use "Abba," we are not only recognizing the closeness we share with God but also expressing our willingness to follow His lead. Jesus' prayer in the Garden captures this perfectly: it is both an intimate moment with His Father and a declaration of submission to God's will, even in the face of great trial.

As you journey through the prayers and reflections in this workbook, you are invited to approach God with the same intimacy and obedience that Jesus modeled. "Abba" is both a term of endearment and a commitment to walk in His ways. It reminds us that our relationship with God is built on love and trust, but also on a willingness to let Him guide our lives, even in difficult moments.

YOU ARE NOT ALONE ON THIS JOURNEY

We often think of Jesus in many different ways—our Savior, our guide, our healer. But how often do we see Him as a friend?

A close, intimate companion who walks with us through life's highs and lows. For some, the idea of a personal friendship with Jesus might feel unfamiliar or distant. We tend to focus on His divinity, His power, and His role as Redeemer, but there's something profoundly special about Jesus inviting us into a relationship that is personal and close.

Jesus longs to be more than a distant figure. **He desires to walk beside you through every season, just like a trusted friend.** A relationship with Jesus involves openness, trust, and the willingness to share your deepest thoughts and emotions. He is always present, always ready to listen, and always ready to extend His love, compassion, and grace.

In this space, you are invited to reflect on what it means to have Jesus as a friend, to experience His companionship in a new and deeper way.

Even in moments when you've felt alone or distant from Him, Jesus has never left your side. The truth is, **He has been walking with you all along—** through joy, pain, uncertainty, and every challenge in between.

Embracing this friendship means allowing Jesus into every part of your life, trusting in His presence, and seeing Him not just as Lord and Savior, but as someone who cares deeply for you.

This journey is about opening your heart to the friendship Jesus offers, building a relationship that is not only deeply personal but also transformative.

Are you willing to lay down your anger at the feet of Jesus?

A JOURNEY OF THE HEART

When I was growing up, one of my favorite poems was 'Footprints in the Sand'. I still remember the first time I heard it—it completely changed the way I thought about Jesus. It was the first time I realized He wasn't just someone far off, watching from a distance. He could be a friend, a companion, someone walking alongside me. That idea stuck with me, even though it took me many more years—four decades, in fact—to really understand just how true it was.

You see, Jesus never left me, even when I felt alone or couldn't see how He was there. And maybe you've felt that too—those times when it doesn't feel like He's close. But the truth is, just because we don't feel it, doesn't mean He isn't there. He's always been there for me, and He's always there for you too. Jesus is that friend who never leaves.

Now, I know that for some of us, we might not have thought of Jesus as a friend before. Maybe you've never spoken to Him like you would with someone close to you. But wouldn't that be something? Just imagine being able to pour out your heart to Him, like you would with your best friend.

So, let's try that together. Let's write to Jesus as the friend He's always been. Think about what you need from Him right now—whether it's comfort, guidance, or just a sense of His presence. What would you ask of a friend? And what can you offer in return?

Write a letter to Jesus, your friend, and tell Him exactly what you need from Him right now and what you're hoping for as you move forward.

Your Fellow Warrior and Journeyman,

FOOTPRINTS IN THE SAND

One night I dreamed I was walking
along the beach with the Lord.
Many scenes from my life flashed across the sky.
In each scene I noticed footprints in the sand.
Sometimes there were two sets of footprints,
other times there were one set of footprints.

This bothered me because I noticed that
during the low periods of my life, when I was
suffering from anguish, sorrow or defeat,
I could see only one set of footprints.

So I said to the Lord, "You promised me
Lord, that if I followed you,
you would walk with me always.
But I have noticed that during the most trying periods
of my life there have only been
one set of footprints in the sand.
Why, when I needed you most,
you have not been there for me?"

The Lord replied,
"The times when you have
seen only one set of footprints,
is when I carried you."

– *Mary Stevenson, 1939*

Dear Jesus,

I've been wanting to write this letter for a few days now, thinking about what to say. I believe this is the first formal friendship letter I've ever written to you. It feels special, and I wish I had done this earlier because it already feels amazing.

Jesus, I'm just learning about you as a friend. I truly didn't believe that was an option for me. I thought you'd be too busy with all you have to do. I didn't think friendship really mattered to you. I thought that was just something those seemingly perfect Christians talked about. But I've just discovered that what you want is friends - not more teachers, prophets, or even warriors, but friends. I can relate to that.

The thought of you wanting to be a friend to me has touched my heart deeply. Now that I've opened my eyes to your offer of friendship, I see that it has been you that has been by my side through my struggling all along.

I want you to know that I am so happy to be your friend, and I won't ignore your calls, your messages, or your subtle hints anymore. I'm still learning how to do this, but I'm truly happy that I've found out you can be more than my healer, counselor, provider, protector, and love - you can also be my friend. That feels really, really good.

I'm grateful for your friendship, and I want to spend a lifetime getting to know you better and sharing who I am with you.

Your Friend,

Kathy

WRITE YOUR LETTER TO JESUS

Write your letter to Jesus, as your friend and comforter, sharing what you need in a best friend. He's ready to listen whenever you're ready to share.

Dear Jesus,

FORGIVENESS: WHAT IT IS, WHAT IT ISN'T

Forgiveness stands as a cornerstone in the foundation of any healthy relationship. Yet, the path to truly forgiving someone can often seem elusive. In this workbook I aim to demystify the process of forgiveness, drawing from personal experiences and a proven approach that has transformed lives, including my own.

Understanding Forgiveness
Forgiveness is more than just a simple declaration; it's a deep, transformative process. Contrary to Webster's sparse definition of forgiveness as "the act of forgiving," I align more closely with a comprehensive view: it involves releasing resentment and the demand for restitution.

What Forgiveness Is Not
To grasp the essence of true forgiveness, we must first clear the misconceptions surrounding it. Forgiveness does not imply forgetting the offense, excusing the behavior, justifying the actions, or endorsing continued poor choices. It's also distinct from reconciliation, which, while a possible outcome, requires the commitment of both parties involved. Forgiveness, in its purest form, requires only the willingness of the forgiver, setting them on a path to personal freedom and healing.

The Misunderstood Advice: Forgive and Forget
Growing up, the counsel to "forgive and forget" was often recited, yet this advice harbors a misleading implication—that remembering an offense equates to holding a grudge. This misconception can trap individuals in a cycle of pain and resentment, hindering genuine forgiveness. True forgiveness involves acknowledging the pain without letting it dictate future relationships or personal well-being.

FORGIVENESS: WHAT IT IS, WHAT IT ISN'T

The Consequences of Unforgiveness
Holding onto unforgiveness can lead to a mirroring of negative traits observed in those who've wronged us, from gossiping to exhibiting passive-aggressive behaviors. This cycle not only affects our personal peace but can sour every interaction, making us prone to taking offense and spreading bitterness. While the process of forgiveness is deeply personal and can be challenging, its rewards are immeasurable. Not only does forgiveness free us from the chains of past hurts, but it also allows us to live with joy and peace, regardless of our circumstances. My hope is that by sharing this process, more people can find the strength to forgive and experience the profound freedom it brings.

Forgiveness without Reconciliation
It's possible to forgive someone without reconciling with them. For example, one might forgive a past wrong to find peace but choose not to engage with the person who caused the harm.

Reconciliation Requires Forgiveness
For true reconciliation to occur, forgiveness is usually a necessary step. It's difficult to rebuild a relationship if one or both parties still harbor significant resentment or anger. Understanding these differences helps in navigating personal and interpersonal conflicts effectively, recognizing when it might be appropriate to focus on personal healing through forgiveness, and when it might be possible or beneficial to pursue reconciliation.

SECTION 2

The Role of Emotions in Forgiveness

In this section, we dive into the role emotions play in the process of forgiveness and healing. Using biblical insights, we explore the complexity of emotions like anger and shame, and introduce tools such as the emotional wheel to help better understand and navigate them.

Through guided prayers and reflections, this section encourages a deeper awareness of how emotions influence our journey toward forgiveness.

THE ROLE OF EMOTIONS IN THE HEALING PROCESS

One of my favorite things about the God we serve is seeing his vast range of responses to the love story between him and his creations.

Embracing emotional authenticity:
Recognizing and validating our emotions is a crucial first step in the forgiveness process. By creating a safe space to honestly confront and express our feelings, whether it's anger, hurt, sadness, or fear, we begin the journey towards healing and wholeness.

Emotions as guides:
Our emotions serve as powerful guides that can lead us towards healing and spiritual growth. By listening to and exploring our emotions, we gain valuable insights into our own needs, wounds, and areas that require God's transformative love and grace.

Healing is a journey:
Emotional healing is a process that requires time, patience, and trust in God's plan. By surrendering our emotions to God and inviting Him into our healing journey, we open ourselves up to deeper levels of forgiveness, restoration, and personal growth.

Forgiveness brings freedom:
Forgiveness is not about condoning wrongdoing or forgetting the pain, but rather about releasing the emotional burden and choosing to let go of resentment. By forgiving others and ourselves, we experience emotional liberation and create space for joy, peace, and love to flourish in our lives.

THE ROLE OF EMOTIONS IN THE HEALING PROCESS

Emotional growth is spiritual growth:
Our emotional experiences, including the challenges of forgiveness, are integral to our spiritual formation and deepening relationship with God. As we navigate the complexities of our emotions and learn to respond with compassion, empathy, and grace, we become more Christlike in our thoughts, words, and actions.

By embracing these key beliefs about the forgiveness process and the significance of our emotions, we embark on a transformative warriors journey of healing, personal growth, and spiritual deepening. As we honor our emotions, seek God's guidance, and choose forgiveness, we open ourselves up to the transformative power of God's love and grace in our lives.

I've put the feeling wheel on the next page because this wheel is pretty fascinating as we go through this journey. It's good to start getting acquainted with your feelings early on. Just observe them and be curious about them. Where on the wheel are you tending to hang out right now? Give yourself some compassion and grace. Know that you are loved.

Remember, the things that happened to you are not your fault. It's not your fault. What happened to you isn't your fault, but it is your job to heal from it and to take accountability for your responses to it.

THE COMPLEX WHEEL OF EMOTIONS

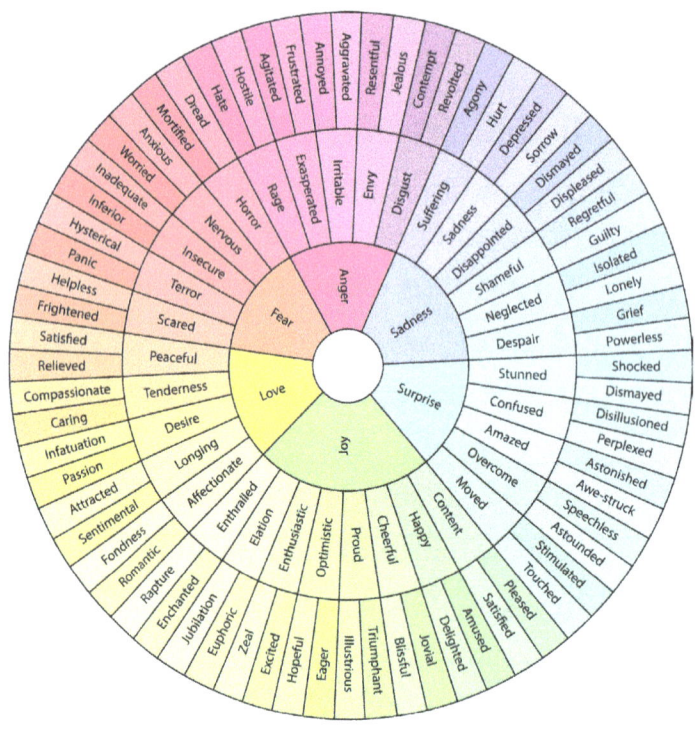

As you start to become aware of the rainbow of feelings connected to the human experience, you may encounter emotions such as:

- Vulnerability, shame, or guilt
- Loneliness, abandonment, or rejection
- Gratitude, contentment, or serenity
- Excitement, anticipation, or curiosity
- Overwhelm, stress, or anxiety
- Empathy, compassion, or love
- Disappointment, frustration, or irritation
- Hope, optimism, or inspiration

By acknowledging and validating the wide range of emotions you experience throughout the forgiveness process, you create space for genuine healing and growth. You learn to embrace the full spectrum of your emotional experience, trusting that God is with you in every moment, guiding you towards greater emotional wholeness and resilience

EMOTIONS IN THE BIBLE

You are in Good Company, let's look at God and some of his emotions as shown the bible.

God Knows our hearts because he created us, let's use this time as a way to enjoy the fruit of our gifts from God who wants us to live a full life.

Anger and Wrath

"The LORD was angry with Solomon because his heart had turned away from the LORD, the God of Israel, who had appeared to him twice." 1 Kings 11:9

Love and Compassion

"The LORD appeared to him from afar, saying, 'I have loved you with an everlasting love; therefore I have drawn you with lovingkindness.'" Jeremiah 31:3

Jealousy

"For you shall not worship any other god, because the LORD, whose name is Jealous, is a jealous God." Exodus 34:14

Grief and Sorrow

"The LORD was sorry that He had made mankind on the earth, and He was grieved in His heart." Genesis 6:6

Hatred

"There are six things that the LORD hates, seven that are an abomination to Him." Proverbs 6:16

EMOTIONS IN THE BIBLE

Joy and Delight

"The LORD your God is in your midst, a victorious warrior. He will rejoice over you with joy, He will be quiet in His love, He will rejoice over you with shouts of joy." Zephaniah 3:17

Pity and Compassion

"Just as a father has compassion on his children, so the LORD has compassion on those who fear Him." Psalm 103:13

Zeal and Passion

"For zeal for Your house has consumed me, and the insults of those who insult You have fallen on me." Psalm 69:9

These verses clearly illustrate that God is portrayed as having a wide range of emotions and feelings, underlining His personal and relational nature.

ANGER: A COMPLEX EMOTION IN CHRISTIAN LIFE

Anger is often viewed as an acceptable sin, one that many Christians struggle with. Scripture teaches us not to sin in our anger and to resolve it quickly, yet we often justify our anger as "righteous." This justification can be dangerous, leading us to compare ourselves favorably to others and potentially sliding into sin.

While anger itself is a natural warning system, designed to prompt us to evaluate our circumstances, it can open doors to harmful behaviors like emotional abuse, self-hatred, bitterness, and unforgiveness. Our culture increasingly normalizes and even celebrates anger, but this acceptance doesn't align with Christian teachings.

The danger lies in allowing anger to linger. When we hold onto anger, it can block our spiritual growth and our ability to hear God's voice. To move forward spiritually, we must acknowledge our pain, fear, and sense of injustice, but then let go of the anger itself.

Think of it like a parent dealing with a toddler's tantrum. The parent's love doesn't diminish, but meaningful communication is impossible until the child calms down. Similarly, God waits patiently for us to be in a state where we can truly listen and connect with Him.

While our anger may seem justified, especially when we've been hurt, holding onto it hinders our relationship with God. To hear His guidance clearly, we must be willing to surrender our anger, offering our pain and fear to Jesus. Only then can we receive the truth He wants to share with us.

Are you willing to give Jesus your anger?

NAVIGATING RIGHTEOUS ANGER

Righteous anger is a type of anger that arises from a sense of injustice or moral wrongdoing. It is driven by a desire to see God's will upheld and to protect the vulnerable. In the Bible, we see examples of righteous anger, such as Jesus overturning the tables of the money changers in the temple (John 2:13-17) or God's anger against sin and oppression (Exodus 32:9-10).

However, it is crucial to recognize that even righteous anger can be misused or corrupted by our sinful nature. We must be cautious not to use the label of "righteous anger" as a way to justify our own selfish or vindictive desires.

To discern between righteous and sinful anger, consider the following:

1. Motive: Righteous anger is driven by a desire for God's justice and righteousness, while sinful anger is often motivated by pride, selfishness, or a desire for personal vengeance.

2. Response: Righteous anger seeks to address the wrong and bring about positive change, while sinful anger often leads to destructive behaviors, such as lashing out, holding grudges, or engaging in verbal or physical abuse.

3. Duration: Righteous anger is typically short-lived and dissipates once the injustice has been addressed, while sinful anger can linger and fester, leading to bitterness and resentment.

4. Fruit: Righteous anger produces godly outcomes, such as reconciliation, restoration, and growth, while sinful anger yields negative consequences, such as division, hurt, and damaged relationships

ASSESSING YOUR ANGER

As you assess your own anger, ask yourself these questions:

- What is the root cause of my anger? Is it truly a matter of injustice or moral wrongdoing, or is it stemming from my own pride or selfish desires?

- How am I expressing my anger? Am I seeking to address the issue constructively, or am I lashing out and causing harm to others?

- How long is my anger lasting? Am I able to let go of it once the situation has been resolved, or am I holding onto bitterness and resentment?

- What are the fruits of my anger? Is it leading to positive change and growth, or is it causing division and damaging my relationships?

By honestly examining our anger in light of these questions, we can begin to discern whether it is righteous or sinful. If we find that our anger is sinful, we must confess it to God, seek His forgiveness, and ask for the Holy Spirit's help in overcoming it.

As Psalm 4:4 reminds us, "Tremble, and do not sin; Meditate in your heart upon your bed, and be still."

SHAME AND FORGIVENESS

The Bible offers extensive wisdom on the topics of shame and forgiveness. Shame and guilt are both self-conscious emotions, but they differ in focus and impact. Shame is a global feeling about oneself, where a person feels inherently flawed or bad as a whole. Guilt, on the other hand, is focused on a specific action or behavior that one regrets. Shame often leads to a desire to hide or disappear, while guilt typically motivates a person to make amends or correct their mistake. Shame is associated with the belief "I am bad," whereas guilt is linked to the thought "I did something bad." Shame tends to be more destructive and can lead to low self-esteem and social withdrawal. Guilt, when not excessive, can be constructive and lead to positive behavioral changes. Understanding this distinction is important for personal growth and maintaining healthy relationships.

Shame is a consequence of sin, but God's love covers shame.
"When I kept silent, my bones wasted away through my groaning all day long. [...] Then I acknowledged my sin to you and did not cover up my iniquity. I said, 'I will confess my transgressions to the Lord.' And you forgave the guilt of my sin." Psalm 32:3,5

Jesus bore our shame on the cross.
"Let us fix our eyes on Jesus, the pioneer and perfecter of faith. For the joy set before him he endured the cross, scorning its shame, and sat down at the right hand of the throne of God." Hebrews 12:2

Forgiveness is a command, not an option.
"Bear with each other and forgive one another if any of you has a grievance against someone. Forgive as the Lord forgave you." Colossians 3:13

Forgiveness brings healing and freedom.
"Therefore confess your sins to each other and pray for each other so that you may be healed." James 5:16

SHAME AND FORGIVENESS

God's forgiveness is complete and permanent.
"For I will forgive their wickedness and will remember their sins no more."
Hebrews 8:12

Forgiveness is an act of love and mercy.
"Be kind and compassionate to one another, forgiving each other, just as in Christ God forgave you." Ephesians 4:32

Unforgiveness can lead to bitterness and resentment.
"See to it that no one falls short of the grace of God and that no bitter root grows up to cause trouble and defile many." Hebrews 12:15

Throughout the Bible, we see that God's love and forgiveness are central themes. By accepting God's forgiveness and extending it to ourselves and others, we can experience the freedom, healing, and restoration that God desires for us. The Bible encourages us to let go of shame and embrace forgiveness as a way to deepen our relationship with God and others.

REFLECT

Let's take a moment to pause and reflect.

Consider your relationship with our Heavenly Father and His Son, Jesus Christ. Do you feel the deep peace, unconditional love, and profound connection that comes from this divine relationship?

I invite you to open your heart to the forgiveness that only Jesus can offer. This forgiveness is a precious gift, freely given through His sacrifice. If you haven't yet embraced this gift for yourself, why not do so now?

Take a deep breath and consider:

Are you carrying burdens that weigh heavily on your soul? Do you long for a sense of peace and release from guilt or shame? Are you ready to accept the love and forgiveness that Jesus offers?

Remember, true forgiveness can only come from the One who bore your punishment.

Jesus, in His infinite love and mercy, has already paid the price for your freedom. All that's left is for you to accept this gift.

PRAY

If you're ready, you can pray something like this:

"Jesus, I acknowledge Your love and sacrifice for me. I accept the forgiveness You offer. Please forgive my sins and help me to live in the freedom and peace of Your love."

or

"Heavenly Father we thank you so much for your Son, Jesus, and Jesus thank you so much for doing what you did for us on the cross, willingly, freely, knowingly, taking our punishment for the sins we did. You took on the burden of our sins and offenses so we didn't have to. We thank you and we love you. I accept the forgiveness that you extend to me by standing in the gap for me, and my sin, so that Heavenly Father sees You, when He looks at me, so that I may be seen as clean and sparkly, white and beautiful. Thank you for standing between us and the wrath we deserve, thank you Jesus for taking the punishment , as a sign of your love for us. I accept forgiveness for all of my sins today."

This moment of acceptance can be the beginning of a transformative journey. As you move forward, know that you are loved, forgiven, and embraced by a Father who delights in you.

May your journey of Love and Understanding and Wisdom come to you and your relationship with the Lord.

SECTION 3

Preparation of the Heart and Mind

Before embarking on the journey of forgiveness, it's essential to prepare your heart and mind for what lies ahead. This process is not a simple one, and it requires you to start by taking inventory of the people and situations that have impacted you. Take a moment to reflect and recognize that forgiveness is not always black and white—it exists on a spectrum, and each step forward is part of the healing process. Through this, we will turn to the Psalms for guidance, expressing our grief and sorrow while allowing God to begin the work of restoration.

STARTING YOUR JOURNEY

As you embark on this journey of forgiveness, understand that this process will require courage, honesty, and a deep reliance on prayer. **Forgiveness is not always easy, but it is a necessary step toward healing and peace.**

To begin, it's important to create a sacred and quiet space for reflection. Find a place where you can play worship music (432 Hz can be a soothing choice), and take time to read comforting Bible passages that remind you of God's promises. Spend a few moments acknowledging who God is—your healer, counselor, provider, Father, and Creator. He is eager to walk this path with you through the Holy Spirit.

Prepare your heart for this journey. Enter into a space of worship and prayer, remembering that you are in God's hands. He is with you every step of the way, wanting nothing more than for you to experience forgiveness, healing, and peace. Trust that His promise is for you to live in wholeness, no matter your circumstances.

> **Once you feel centered and connected, we will begin by taking an inventory of your heart.**

With the Holy Spirit's guidance, reflect on the people, organizations, or institutions that have caused you harm or triggered feelings of resentment or pain. This is not a time for deep reflection on what happened—simply make a list of those that come to mind. Trust the process, and know that this is where your journey begins.

FORGIVENESS INVENTORY

Create a list of people, organizations, and situations that trigger feelings of offense or resentment within you. Ensuring a comprehensive inventory is crucial.

A MOMENT TO REFLECT

Now that we've completed the inventory, take a moment to reflect.

This is a significant step, and you may start to feel various emotions in your body. This is perfectly normal, which is why I've provided the feeling wheel. You can start idenitfying what triggers and feelings are moving you. This wheel is a fascinating tool that we'll use throughout our journey, and it's beneficial to become familiar with your feelings early on.

Be curious about your emotions and simply observe them without judgment. Where on the wheel do your current feelings tend to cluster? Offer yourself compassion and grace, remembering that you are loved. What happened to you is not your fault, but healing from it and taking accountability for your responses is your responsibility.

Next, we'll move on to the following worksheet. On the next page, you'll see a colorful spectrum. This is to remind you that forgiveness, like grief, isn't a linear process. The old paradigm of five stages of grief has been rejected by healing communities because both grief and forgiveness tend to have varied degrees and don't follow a straight path.

We're going to map a few names on this spectrum to give you a visual representation of where you currently stand in your forgiveness journey with these close relationships. This exercise will help you understand your progress and identify areas where you might need to focus more attention.

FORGIVENESS IS NOT BLACK AND WHITE

In this exercise, we will explore where you currently stand in your close relationships by mapping out a few key names on a spectrum. Begin by identifying five or six of the most impactful relationships in your life that need repair or possibly letting go. On the next page, write down their names, reflecting on where your heart currently feels about each relationship.

Once you have your list, consider where each person fits on this spectrum.

Are you at the stage of just acknowledging the hurt? Are you recognizing that what happened was wrong? That's a significant first step. Or, are you trying to seek understanding about why this person acted the way they did? Are you considering their perspective and the other side of the story? Use this mapping to gain insight into your emotional state and the nature of these relationships.

1. Acknowledging the brokenness: You honestly face the pain and hurt caused by the offense, recognizing that we live in a fallen world where people can wound one another. You bring your emotions and struggles to God in prayer, seeking His comfort and guidance.

2. Reflecting on God's mercy: You reflect on your own need for God's forgiveness and the countless times He has shown mercy to you. You acknowledge that just as God has forgiven you through Christ, you are called to extend forgiveness to others.

3. Choosing to forgive: You make a deliberate choice to forgive the person who hurt you, not based on your feelings, but in obedience to God's command to forgive others as He has forgiven you (Ephesians 4:32). You trust that God will give you the strength to forgive.

4. Praying for understanding and compassion: You ask God to help you see the other person through His eyes and to give you a heart of compassion. You pray for the other person's well-being and for God to work in their life, recognizing that they, too, are in need of God's grace and transformation.

5. Releasing the offense to God: You surrender the hurt and the offense to God, trusting Him to bring justice and healing in His perfect timing. You release the burden of unforgiveness, allowing God to carry the weight and trusting Him to work all things together for good (Romans 8:28).

6. Blessing and the Lessons - and in interceding: As an act of love and obedience to God, you pray blessings over the person who hurt you. You intercede for their spiritual growth, asking God to transform their heart and draw them closer to Himself. You trust that as you bless and pray for them, God will continue to heal and transform your own heart as well.

Throughout this process, you continually seek God's guidance, strength, and love, recognizing that true forgiveness is only possible through the power of the Holy Spirit working within you.

You trust that as you walk in forgiveness, God will deepen your faith, heal your wounds, and use your experiences to minister to others who are struggling to forgive.

He promises.

THE SPECTRUM OF FORGIVENESS

Spend a few minutes mapping out your current status with your closet relationships to uncover your true state of forgiveness.

Acknowledging the Hurt	Seeking Understanding	Choosing to Forgive	Praying for Understanding and Forgiveness	Releasing the Offense to God	Blessing and Interceding

LAMENTING THROUGH PSALM

Jesus experienced the full range of human emotions and trials. He was betrayed, abandoned, rejected, misunderstood, and wrongly accused. He knows what it's like to have pain caused by others' actions. Yet, in His deepest agony, He found the strength to pray, "Father, forgive them, for they do not know what they are doing."

Those who hurt us often can't comprehend the long-lasting ripple effects of their actions - the consequences we still feel years, even decades, after the transgression. Sadly sometimes the person who hurt us the most is ourselves.

This brings us to our next activity: writing our own psalm of lament. Laments are a form of expression found throughout the Bible, particularly in the book of Psalms. Psalms are ancient Hebrew poems and hymns, many of which were written by King David. They cover a wide range of human experiences and emotions, from joy and praise to deep sorrow and anger.

The purpose of Psalms in our lives is multifaceted:

- They provide a model for honest communication with God.
- They offer comfort and reassurance in difficult times.
- They help us express our deepest emotions, both positive and negative.
- They remind us of God's faithfulness throughout history.

As you write your own psalm of lament, remember this song or prayer is addressed to God, focusing on the theme of forgiving those who don't realize the impact of their actions. Like many biblical psalms, your lament can express your pain, frustration, and desire for justice, while ultimately turning towards trust in God and the path of forgiveness.

This exercise allows you to pour out your heart to God, just as the psalmists did, and to process your emotions in a constructive, faith-centered way.

PREPARING YOUR HEART TO LAMENT

Before you begin writing your own psalm of lament, I want to share an example of what this can look like. This is a personal reflection—a heartfelt prayer that mirrors the psalms found in Scripture. It expresses raw emotions, feelings of pain, and the longing for justice, while ultimately seeking God's guidance and strength to forgive.

As you read this example, **remember that there is no "right" or "wrong" way to write your own lament**. This is an intimate, deeply personal expression of your heart before God. The key is to be honest about your pain, open about your struggles, and, like the psalmists, turn your focus towards God's faithfulness and His power to heal and restore.

May this example inspire you as you pour out your own heart to the One who understands your suffering and invites you to walk the path of forgiveness and healing.

As you'll notice, this example ends with the word *Selah*. This ancient term, found throughout the Psalms, holds deep significance. Though its exact meaning is debated, many believe Selah invites us to pause, reflect, and meditate on what has just been said. **It is a powerful reminder to take a breath and let the words sink in, allowing space for God's presence to meet us in the silence.**

Ending your psalm with *Selah* encourages you to stop and truly feel the weight of the emotions, the pain, and ultimately, the release you've expressed. It's a moment of stillness—an invitation to trust that God has heard your lament and is at work in your healing, even if the resolution is not yet clear.

In the midst of our deepest struggles and prayers, *Selah* calls us to rest in the assurance of God's faithfulness.

A PSALM OF FORGIVENESS AND GROWTH

O Lord, You plant seeds of compassion within us, Nurturing a heart that balances understanding with truth. In Your wisdom, You show us the path of forgiveness, Where healing and accountability walk hand in hand.

When we falter, dear Father, You embrace us, Your forgiveness flowing through our very being. Let us mirror Your grace in our daily lives, Creating ripples of trust and openness wherever we go.

Remind us, O God, that forgiveness is not blindness, But a clear-eyed vision of Your redemptive love. Help us hold fast to Your standards of goodness, While extending the same mercy You've shown us.

Grant us the gift of empathy, Lord of all understanding, To see through the eyes of those around us. For in glimpsing their hearts, we glimpse Yours, And our relationships become acts of love.

In moments of failure, whisper to us, O Lord of my Heart, That every stumble is a step towards growth. Let not judgment be my first response, But rather a curiosity for what can be learned.

As I journey on this path of forgiveness, May my actions echo Your divine grace. In forgiving, may I be reminded of my own forgiveness, In understanding, may we be understood.

For in Your infinite wisdom, You've shown me That true strength lies in compassion, True power in forgiveness, And true growth in love.

Amen.

CREATE YOUR PSALM TO GOD

SECTION 4

Starting the Forgiveness Journey

As you step into the forgiveness journey, it's time to focus on a specific person from your list. Reflect on what they did and how their actions caused you pain. Take the time to identify what you feel is still owed to you and the emotional wounds that remain. In this space of reflection, also consider how their hurt may have shaped your own actions and responses, even those that may not reflect your true character.

This is where the journey toward healing truly begins.

Note: Whenever you encounter this symbol later in the book, please return to the indicated section to explore forgiveness related to your new insights and discoveries.

EXPLORING FORGIVENESS

Let's begin. Choose one person from your list for our first detailed exploration.

Delve into the specifics: What did they do? How did they hurt you?

Be specific and thorough. This is your opportunity to express everything, leaving no room for unresolved feelings or negative influences to linger or strongholds to take effect.

WHAT DO YOU FEEL YOU ARE OWED?

Next, **reflect on what you feel they owe you**. Is it time that was lost? Is it money or financial support? Consider what you would want to get back if you could. Write down these thoughts in detail. This can help you clarify your feelings and articulate what you need for healing.

Take this time to write out your thoughts to God. Share with Him the pain you've experienced, the specifics of what happened, and what you believe you are owed.

This act of writing can be a powerful step in your journey toward forgiveness and healing.

WHAT DO YOU FEEL YOU ARE OWED?

IDENTIFY THE PAIN

Every offense stems from a hurt: Circle or highlight the emotions that you feel best describe the pain you've experienced.

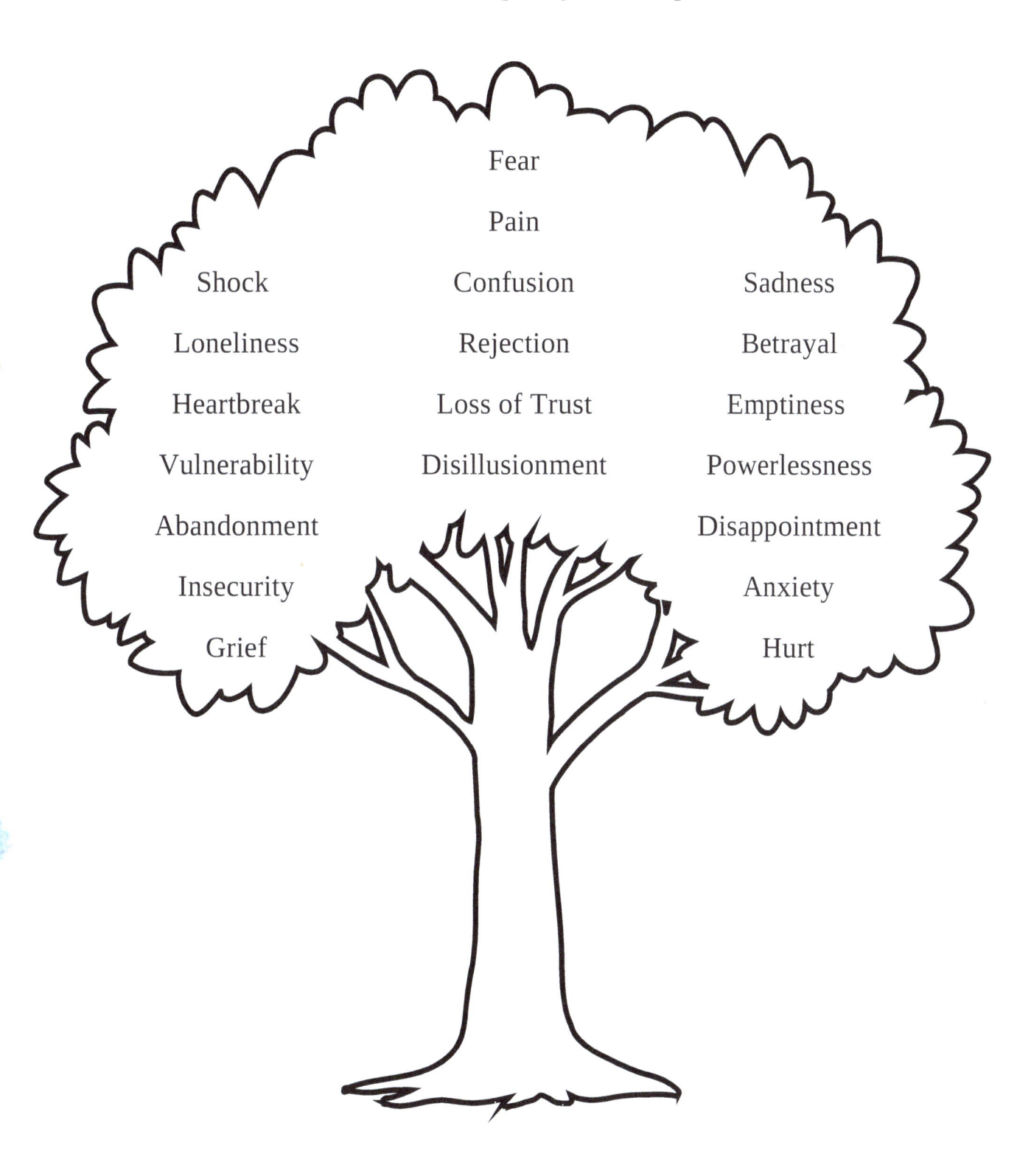

Fear
Pain
Shock Confusion Sadness
Loneliness Rejection Betrayal
Heartbreak Loss of Trust Emptiness
Vulnerability Disillusionment Powerlessness
Abandonment Disappointment
Insecurity Anxiety
Grief Hurt

OWNING OUR REACTIONS

Now is the time to take an honest inventory of our responses to the offense.

As we proceed, allow the Holy Spirit to guide you towards truth and self-awareness. Remember, while you had no control over the actions taken against you, you are responsible for your reactions, assuming you're of an age to be accountable.

This truth often makes forgiveness challenging. Regardless of how unjust or severe your treatment was, the pain it caused likely triggered responses that further disconnected you - not only from the person who hurt you, but potentially from others and even yourself.

In my own journey, I've found that unresolved hurt often led to poor life choices. I overspent, overindulged, neglected responsibilities, gossiped about those who hurt me, and justified my lingering anger. From experience, I can attest that such behaviors only breed bitterness and resentment.

Holding onto unforgiveness can permeate various aspects of your life, potentially making you hypersensitive to offense and more susceptible to discontent. However, recognizing these patterns is the first step towards healing and freedom.

As we continue, remember that this process isn't about assigning blame, but about understanding our responses so we can move towards forgiveness and emotional health.

As you go through the next six pages, reflect on your reactions and circle any responses that resonate with your experience—whether communication issues, emotional states, negative thoughts, harmful actions, or unhealthy coping mechanisms.

COMMUNICATION ISSUES

As you reflect on your reactions to the situation, circle any communication issues that describe how you expressed yourself or interacted with others.

Lust	Strife
Dissension	Relationship Problems
Factions	Cynicism
Emotional Numbness	Insults
Arguments	Stonewalling
Yelling	Verbal Abuse
Misunderstandings	Sarcasm
Impatience	Bitterness
Passive-Aggressive Social Media Posts	Unforgiveness
Difficulty Trusting Others	Passive-Aggressive Humor

EMOTIONAL STATES

As you reflect on your reactions to the situation, circle any emotional states that resonate with how you felt during and after the experience.

Depression	Confusion	Hatred
Loneliness	Unworthiness	Self-Guilt
Fear	Envy	Condemnation
Insecurity	Jealousy	Overly Sensitive
Anxiety	Self-Hate	Emotional Numbness
Discontent	Hopelessness	Overwhelmed
Anger	Shame	Frustrated
Disgust	Lack of Self-Esteem	Discouraged
Feelings of Inadequacy	Doubt and Unbelief Toward God	

NEGATIVE THOUGHT PATTERNS

As you reflect on your reactions to the situation, circle any negative thought patterns that describe how you perceived or processed the experience.

Psuedo Guilt	Critical of Others	People-Pleasing
Easily Offended	Denial	Neediness
Rebellion	Worry	Opinionated
Victimization	Disgust	Unbelief
Self-Righteousness	Holding Grudges	Superiority Complex
Self-Pity	Pessimism	False Humility
Racism	Cynicism	Legalism
Suspicion	Complaining	Spiritual Pride
Unforgiving of Self	Negativity	Obsessive Thinking
Resentment	Self-Protection	Fortune-Telling
Defensiveness	Thoughts of Revenge	Rumination
Envy	Self-Centered Thoughts	Idolatry of Self (Pride)
Suspicion		Difficulty Forgiving Oneself
Justifying Unloving Behavior	Difficulty Accepting Constructive Criticism	Doubting God's Goodness
Unforgiving of Others		

UNHEALTHY COPING MECHANISMS

As you reflect on your reactions to the situation, circle any unhealthy coping mechanisms you used to manage your emotions or the experience.

Drunkenness	Codependency	Perfectionism
Drug Use	Pornography	Emotional Eating
Workaholism	Smut Novels	Excessive Sleep
Materialism	Gambling	Retail Therapy
Overspending	Procrastination	Sex
Laziness	Avoidance	Addiction
Obsessive Actions	Self-Harm	Excessive Exercise
Compulsive Behaviors	Emotional Detachment	Witchcraft
Escaping Through Activity	Thrill-Seeking Behavior	Idol Worship (Celebrity)

HARMFUL ACTIONS

As you reflect on your reactions to the situation, circle any harmful actions that describe how you responded or acted toward others or yourself.

Retaliation	Revengeful Actions	Bigotry
Seeking Revenge	Coldheartedness	Abortion
Inconsideration	Childish Behavior	Murder
Insubordination	Unkindness	Greed
Lying	Negative Speech	Stinginess
Disobedience	Demanding Justice	Unloving Behavior
Controlling Behavior	Abuse	Stubbornness
Gluttony	Self-Seeking Behavior	Manipulation
Overeating	Nagging	Hard-Headedness
Vanity	Ungratefulness	Hard-Heartedness
Violence	Profanity	Sharp Tongue
Causing Strife	Malicious Communication	Wastefulness
Touchiness		Prejudice
Defiance Against Authority	Setting Others Up for Failure	Poor Stewardship of Money
Keeping a List of Wrongs	Elevating People Over God	Cyberbullying and Online Harassment

HARMFUL ACTIONS (CONTINUED)

Mercilessness	Entitlement	Blaming Others
Dishonesty	Betrayal	Rejection
Rudeness	Unrepentance	Adultery
Judgmentalism	Silent Treatment	Teasing
False Worship	Blame-Shifting	Taunting
Gossip	Gaslighting	Stealing
Isolation	Slander	Passive-Aggressive Behavior
Overeating	False Witness	Causing Others to Stumble
Vanity	Emotional Manipulation	Setting Others Up for Failure
Violence	Sabotaging Others' Success	Withholding Love and Affection
Causing Strife	Holding Onto Things God Has Instructed to Let Go	Withdrawing From People
Blasphemy		
Touchiness		
Loving Something or Someone More Than God	Elevating Situations or Material Items Over God	
Shirking Responsibility	Hiding From Relationships	Withdrawing From Community

Shine God's Light on your past.

Let it go.

Give it to Him.

PRAY

As we begin this guided prayer, please have your completed pages with you.

Dear Heavenly Father (Abba),

I admit I have sinned against Your Spirit, by not forgiving those who hurt me, and I recognize that I have taken on sins from the offenses of *(Name the Person)*. I didn't even realize I was carrying all these around. I acknowledge my inability and desire to forgive them, apart from You. <u>I ask You now to grant me a repentant and forgiving, softened heart.</u>

I believe by faith, and confess my sins before You. Since You have already forgiven me, I am now going to receive that forgiveness for each and every one of my sins that disconnected me from You and others.
(Name off each one of the responses you circled and finish each one with the words "I am forgiven.")

I thank You now for forgiving me, cleansing me, and setting me free, as only You can. I am now free to forgive myself. Jesus, I ask You now to heal my broken heart, and my feelings of *(Name the words you circled from the tree activity)*.

I am willing to lay down my anger to You, Jesus, for all of the wrong they have done to me; they no longer owe me anything. *(List what you feel they owed you.)*

I will trust You to restore all that is needed in my life because You know all that my heart desires and all of my needs. I pray that only Your love will fill in all these areas the sins and hurt left behind, so there is no room for them to return. Father, if they do return, I know that I can simply confess them to You, as Your love is unconditional, and I can come to You as often as needed to stay clean; and my desire is to live as a person who forgives.

I ask You to reconcile this relationship in my heart, and reconcile Your heart to mine. I ask that You will bless them and lead them to a closer relationship with You.

In Jesus' name, Amen.

REFLECT

Take a moment to check in with yourself. How do you feel now?

If you feel peace, cherish this gift. When our Heavenly Father heals, He heals completely and eternally. This peace is a testament to His work in your heart.

If you feel grief, know that this is a natural and common response.

Often, it's the fear of confronting our grief that holds us back from beginning the forgiveness process. Grief is a complex emotion that deserves its own space and attention. We'll explore this topic more deeply in a future workbook and teaching. We have some self care ideas in the back to honor your body and heart and minds response today.

Remember, whatever you're feeling is valid. This process is a journey, and each step forward is progress, even if it doesn't always feel that way. Be patient and gentle with yourself as you navigate these emotions.

Grief and forgiveness go hand in hand. It is natural and healthy to feel this, **call on God the Comforter and Healer**.

SECTION 5

Navigating Grief in Forgiveness

Grief and forgiveness are intertwined aspects of the healing journey, each playing a vital role in our emotional and spiritual well-being. As we navigate the depths of our sorrow, we may find ourselves grappling with feelings of anger, resentment, and unresolved pain.

This section invites you to explore how embracing grief can pave the way for genuine forgiveness, not only toward others but also toward ourselves. By acknowledging our emotions and allowing ourselves to grieve, we create space for healing and transformation. Join us as we delve into the process of navigating grief in the context of forgiveness, discovering the profound freedom that comes from reconciling our past and moving toward a hopeful future.

THE INTERSECTION OF GRIEF AND FORGIVENESS

In His final moments on the cross, Jesus spoke words that echo through time:

"Father, forgive them, for they know not what they do."

In this profound act, Jesus released all control and embodied the essence of unconditional forgiveness. It was more than just pardoning those who wronged Him—it was a spiritual surrender, a letting go of pain, and an invitation for divine power to take over. Through this, **He showed us that forgiveness is not just about excusing someone's actions; it's about entrusting our deepest hurts to God.**

Forgiveness is often seen as the path to healing, but many struggle with taking that first step. This hesitation isn't always rooted in stubbornness or a desire for revenge. Often, it's a response to something much deeper: **the fear of confronting hidden grief.**

Forgiveness and grief are intricately connected, especially when dealing with disenfranchised losses—those losses that society doesn't acknowledge, validate, or support. Grief from these overlooked losses can block the ability to forgive, because the thought of facing the underlying sadness can feel overwhelming. Subconsciously, we may cling to anger or resentment as a way to avoid the vulnerability that grief demands.

When we are unable to forgive, it's not just the offense we hold on to, but also the unprocessed grief tied to that pain. As Jesus demonstrated on the cross, the power of forgiveness is found in surrendering—not just the wrongs done to us, but the weight of our own sorrow.

By releasing this burden, we allow healing to begin.

FINDING FALSE SECURITY IN UNFORGIVENESS

Unforgiveness often acts as a defense mechanism, shielding us from facing the full extent of our pain. For many, anger feels like a safe harbor, providing a sense of control over a situation that has left them feeling vulnerable. Yet beneath this anger often lies unresolved grief, a hidden sorrow that we may not be ready to confront.

For some, **clinging to anger feels like a way of maintaining a connection to what was lost, an illusion of power in a landscape marked by loss.** Others may hesitate to forgive because doing so feels akin to accepting the reality of that loss, which can be terrifying. In this way, unforgiveness becomes a false security blanket, offering comfort in its familiarity while obscuring the healing that can come from facing our grief.

This false sense of security manifests in several ways. First, it allows us to avoid vulnerability. Anger can create a protective barrier, making us feel strong and in control, while grief lays bare our fragility. We may also find ourselves maintaining a connection to the past through resentment, convinced that our anger keeps the memory of what we lost alive. Additionally, **the act of postponing acceptance becomes a coping mechanism; by staying angry, we can avoid the painful truth of our loss.**

"There is a way which seems right to a man, but its end is the way of death." (Proverbs 14:12)

This verse highlights the danger of finding false security in unforgiveness, reminding us that what feels right in the moment may lead to harmful outcomes.

By understanding the false security it provides, we can begin to unravel the threads of anger and grief, opening ourselves to the possibility of true forgiveness and the profound freedom that follows.

INTEGRATING GRIEF AND FORGIVENESS

It's important to **remember that grief and forgiveness are not opposing forces**; in fact, they often work together on the path to healing. By allowing ourselves to grieve, we create space for forgiveness—not just of others, but also of ourselves and the circumstances surrounding our loss. This integration is essential because **true healing requires acknowledging the depth of our emotions.**

Grief, in its many forms, is a natural response to loss. It encompasses a range of feelings, including sadness, anger, confusion, and even relief. These emotions are valid and deserve to be felt. Forgiveness, on the other hand, is an intentional choice that can facilitate healing. It is the act of releasing the hold that pain and resentment have over us. When we allow ourselves to experience grief, we begin to untangle the knots that unforgiveness has tied around our hearts.

As you move through this process, give yourself grace. Healing is not a linear journey; it's okay to ebb and flow between anger, grief, and forgiveness. You might find that certain days are heavier than others, or that triggers unexpectedly surface old wounds. This is part of the journey. Each emotion, each step—no matter how small—brings you closer to peace and wholeness. Embrace the messiness of healing, knowing that every feeling is a sign of your courage to confront the depths of your heart.

"For I know the plans that I have for you," declares the Lord, *"plans for welfare and not for calamity to give you a future and a hope."* (Jeremiah 29:11)

This promise reminds us that God's plan for us is one of hope, healing, and wholeness. As we navigate the journey of forgiveness, even when it feels safer to stay in our pain, we can trust that God is leading us toward peace and restoration.

SHARING YOUR GRIEF WITH GOD

Some grief must be shared to be healed. Take this time to write a letter to our Heavenly Father, expressing your sorrow and burdens. Consider the following prompts to guide your thoughts:

Begin with an Opening
Start your letter by addressing God in a way that feels comfortable for you. You might say, "Dear God," "Heavenly Father," or simply "Lord."

Express Your Emotions
Pour out your heart—share the specifics of your grief. What are the pain points that weigh heavily on you? What memories or feelings resurface as you write? Allow yourself to be vulnerable in this space.

Ask for Comfort
Invite Jesus, your Comforter, into your pain. What do you need from Him right now? Ask for His presence, guidance, and strength to navigate this healing journey.

End with Hope
Conclude your letter by expressing hope for healing and renewal. You might include a prayer or a statement of trust in God's plans for your future.

After writing your letter, consider reading it aloud in prayer. This act of sharing your grief can be a powerful step in releasing burdens and inviting divine comfort into your life.

SHARING YOUR GRIEF WITH GOD

SCRIPTURES OF COMFORT AND HEALING

These verses reveal God's compassionate nature as the source of true comfort and healing. Whether we are afflicted, brokenhearted, or weary, God's merciful love and the Holy Spirit's presence provide the healing our hearts and spirits need.

Let these Scriptures remind you that the Lord is near to those who suffer and binds up every wound, offering rest and restoration to all who seek Him.

Isaiah 51:12
"I, even I, am he who comforts you."

2 Corinthians 1:3-4
"Blessed be the God and Father of our Lord Jesus Christ, the Father of mercies and God of all comfort, who comforts us in all our affliction..."

Psalm 147:3
"He heals the brokenhearted and binds up their wounds."

Exodus 15:26
"...I am the LORD who heals you."

John 14:16,26
"And I will pray the Father, and He will give you another Comforter...the Comforter, the Holy Spirit..."

Psalm 34:18
"The LORD is near to the brokenhearted and saves the crushed in spirit."

A LETTER OF COMPASSION

Write a compassionate letter to your past self, acknowledging both the pain and the growth that have shaped you. Reflect on the following prompts to guide your writing:

Address Your Past Self
Start by addressing yourself as you were during a difficult time. You might use your name or a term of endearment, like "Dear [Your Name]," or "My dear heart."

Acknowledge the Pain
Recognize the challenges and hardships you faced. What specific moments caused you pain? Allow yourself to validate those feelings without judgment.

Celebrate Your Growth
Reflect on how you've changed and grown since those times. What lessons have you learned? How have your experiences shaped you into the person you are today?

Offer Understanding and Forgiveness
Extend compassion to your past self. Understand that every choice was made within the context of your experiences and emotions. Forgive yourself for any perceived mistakes, acknowledging that you did the best you could with what you knew at the time.

Encourage Your Present Self
Conclude your letter with encouragement. Celebrate your progress and resilience. Remind yourself of the strength and hope that lies ahead.

After completing your letter, consider keeping it somewhere safe as a reminder of your journey. You might choose to read it again in the future to reflect on how far you've come and to reignite your compassion for yourself.

A LETTER OF COMPASSION

SECTION 6

Embracing God's Truth

In this section, you'll explore the concept of lie-based thinking and how it can negatively influence your emotions and beliefs. Through a guided process, you'll learn to identify and address the unsettled feelings that arise from false beliefs, replacing them with the truth found in scripture.

With verses that encourage growth, strength, and resilience through adversity, this section empowers you to break free from harmful thought patterns and embrace a renewed mindset grounded in God's truth.

ARE YOU FEELING UNSETTLED?

The concept of "lie-based thinking," as discussed in Dr. Ed Smith's book, *Healing Life's Hurts*, refers to the idea that our thoughts and beliefs can be shaped by lies or distortions we've come to accept over time. These false beliefs often stem from past hurts, misunderstandings, or painful experiences and can lead to negative emotions, behaviors, and broken relationships. When we believe these lies—such as the idea that we are unworthy of love, incapable of change, or undeserving of forgiveness—it can trap us in a cycle of resentment and bitterness.

Forgiveness plays a crucial role in breaking this cycle. By forgiving others, and ourselves, we begin to challenge these distorted thoughts and replace them with truth. Forgiveness allows us to release the false narratives that keep us bound to the pain of the past. It opens the door to healing, enabling us to see ourselves and others as worthy of love, grace, and compassion. By addressing lie-based thinking, we can free ourselves from the grip of negative emotions and restore healthier relationships—both with others and within our own hearts.

Understanding Lie-Based Thinking

Lie-based thinking stems from internalizing lies or distortions about ourselves, others, or God. These lies can come from various sources, such as past experiences, societal influences, or even our own negative self-talk. They can lead to distorted beliefs and thought patterns that affect our emotions and actions.

Examples of Lie-Based Thinking

"I'm not good enough."
" I am unlovable."
"I am worthless."

HOW TO ADDRESS LIE-BASED THINKING

Identify the Lies
Begin by becoming aware of the negative thoughts and false beliefs that are influencing your emotions and behaviors. These lies often stem from past hurts or experiences and can distort your perception of yourself, others, and God.

Replace Lies with Truth
Challenge these lies by replacing them with truth, drawn from God's Word and sound reasoning. Ask Jesus to speak His truth into your heart. Present the lie to Him, ask for His truth, then take time to be quiet, still, and listen. Let His truth guide your life, not the lies.

Renew Your Mind
Continuously renew your mind by meditating on and internalizing the truth (Romans 12:2). Make it a daily practice to focus on God's Word and let it reshape your thoughts, beliefs, and actions.

Seek Support
Don't face this journey alone. Seek guidance from trusted individuals, counselors, or mentors who can help you recognize and overcome lie-based thinking. Having support and accountability can help you stay rooted in truth and avoid slipping back into old thought patterns.

The key to overcoming lie-based thinking is to identify the lies, replace them with God's truth, and continuously renew your mind with the truth. This process involves actively challenging negative thoughts and beliefs and intentionally replacing them with biblical principles and sound reasoning.

SCRIPTURES FOR EMBRACING TRUTH AND A NEW LIFE

As we confront the lies we've carried, particularly those that fuel guilt and self-condemnation, strong emotions often surface. These scriptures remind us of the power of truth to break those lies and set us free. By renewing our minds with God's Word, we can release the false beliefs that hold us back and embrace self-forgiveness.

Let these verses guide you in replacing deception with truth and finding peace as you journey toward healing and wholeness.

The Power of Truth - John 8:32
"And you will know the truth, and the truth will make you free."

Renewing Your Mind - Ephesians 4:22-24
"That, in reference to your former manner of life, you lay aside the old self, which is being corrupted in accordance with the lusts of deceit, and that you be renewed in the spirit of your mind, and put on the new self, which in the likeness of God has been created in righteousness and holiness of the truth."

Focusing on What is Good - Philippians 4:8
"Finally, brothers and sisters, whatever is true, whatever is honorable, whatever is right, whatever is pure, whatever is lovely, whatever is commendable, if there is any excellence and if anything worthy of praise, think about these things."

SCRIPTURES ON GROWTH AND STRENGTH THROUGH ADVERSITY

God's sovereignty shines through in His ability to bring good from even the most difficult situations. Through trials and afflictions, He refines our character, strengthens our faith, and works everything for our ultimate good. Trusting in Him allows us to see challenges not as setbacks, but as opportunities for growth, endurance, and transformation guided by His loving hand.

Good from All Things - Romans 8:28
"And we know that God causes all things to work together for good to those who love God, to those who are called according to His purpose."

Turning Evil into Good - Genesis 50:20
"As for you, you meant evil against me, but God meant it for good in order to bring about this present result, to preserve many people alive."

Suffering Has Eternal Value - 2 Corinthians 4:17
"For momentary, light affliction is producing for us an eternal weight of glory far beyond all comparison."

Endurance and Growth - James 1:2-4
"Consider it all joy, my brethren, when you encounter various trials, knowing that the testing of your faith produces endurance. And let endurance have its perfect result, so that you may be perfect and complete, lacking in nothing."

Hope - Jeremiah 29:11
"'For I know the plans that I have for you,' declares the Lord, 'plans for welfare and not for calamity to give you a future and a hope.'"

PRAY

This guided prayer offers a chance to thank God for the freedom and healing that come from embracing His truth. It also invites His continued guidance as we grow through challenges and stay rooted in His grace.

Dear Heavenly Father (Abba),

I come before You with a heart overflowing with gratitude. Thank You for teaching me the lesson of accepting forgiveness for myself and for revealing the lies I've unknowingly carried for so long. These false beliefs have weighed heavily on my spirit, affecting my emotions, actions, and relationships. But in Your abundant grace and mercy, You have shown me the truth, and I praise You for the freedom that comes from being rooted in Your Word.

Lord, I thank You for Your incredible ability to bring good out of even the most difficult situations. When I face trials, You are there, using them to shape and grow me in ways I couldn't imagine. You never waste my pain. Through each challenge, You are developing my character, refining my heart, and strengthening my faith. I see now that my journey through accepting forgiveness for myself is part of this growth, and I trust that You are using it for my good.

As I continue on this path, I ask for Your guidance. Help me to release the lies that have held me captive and to stay firmly grounded in the truth of who You say I am. Let Your Word fill my heart and mind, replacing the negative thoughts and deceptions that have kept me from fully embracing Your love and forgiveness.

When I struggle, when old wounds resurface or when I find it hard to forgive myself or others, remind me of Your promise that Your truth sets me free. Help me to trust You more deeply, knowing that through every trial, You are working in me to produce endurance, hope, and a character that reflects Your goodness.

Father, I commit to seeking Your truth each day and to allowing it to shape my life. May I walk in the freedom, peace, and joy that You have for me, trusting that You are with me every step of the way.

In Jesus' name, Amen.

REFLECT

Take a quiet moment to reflect on the path you've traveled in embracing God's truth and accepting forgiveness for yourself.

Think about how God has been working in your heart, helping you confront the lies that once weighed heavily on your spirit. Are you beginning to feel lighter, more at peace as you walk in His truth?

God offers you the gift of freedom from false beliefs and self-condemnation. It's a gift freely given through His grace and love. If you've been holding onto burdens from the past, consider opening your heart to release them fully into His hands.

Ask yourself:

Are there lingering thoughts or feelings that still keep you from experiencing true peace? What would it feel like to let go of these lies and embrace the truth of who God says you are?

God's love is constant, and His truth brings lasting freedom.

Trust that God, who transforms every trial into an opportunity for growth, is offering you the peace and release you seek. Will you let go of what holds you back and fully receive the healing He offers?

SECTION 7

The Labels That Define Us

In this section, you will explore the profound impact that labels—whether given by others or accepted by yourself—can have on your life. By recognizing the harm of these negative labels, you'll begin the process of confronting and challenging the ways they have shaped your identity.

As you continue, you will discover the truth of who God says you are. Through guided activities and reflection, you'll learn to embrace the empowering labels God places on you, reclaim your true identity, and walk in the freedom of your divine worth.

UNDERSTANDING THE POWER OF LABELS

Romans 12:2 reminds us, *"And do not be conformed to this world, but be transformed by the renewing of your mind, so that you may prove what the will of God is, that which is good and acceptable and perfect."*

This verse calls us to reject the labels and judgments placed upon us by the world and instead embrace the transformation that comes through the renewing of our minds in Christ. **Worldly labels can deeply affect us, shaping our identity in ways that lead to feelings of inadequacy, shame, and self-doubt.** These false labels, rooted in the world's limited perspective, can prevent us from seeing ourselves as God sees us.

These labels can often stem from painful experiences—hurtful words spoken over us, societal stereotypes, or even our own internal self-criticism. When we allow these negative labels to define us, we may carry burdens of unforgiveness toward others and even toward ourselves. But God's truth is far more powerful than any label the world could place on us.

He calls us loved, chosen, and redeemed.

The journey of forgiveness begins with releasing not only the hurtful actions of others but also the harmful labels we have allowed to shape our identity.

In this section, we will confront the harmful labels that have impacted our lives. Through reflection and the power of God's truth, you will begin to let go of the labels that have weighed you down and step into the freedom of forgiveness—both for others and for yourself. **This is a journey of releasing what the world says and embracing the identity God has given you.** As you renew your mind with His truth, you'll find healing and transformation, leaving behind the false labels and stepping into the fullness of who you are in Christ.

IDENTIFYING HARMFUL LABELS

As you read through this list of examples, take a moment to listen to your heart and see if any of these resonate with you. These labels, often picked up through negative self-talk, hurtful words from others, or societal stereotypes, may have shaped how you see yourself.

Unworthy	Useless	Invisible
Failure	Burden	Annoying
Unlovable	Irresponsible	Problematic
Weak	Unwanted	Defective
Stupid	Disappointing	Worthless
Broken	Pathetic	Dumb
Ugly	Coward	Inferior
Lazy	Insecure	Unsuccessful
Not Good Enough	Loser	Damaged

CONFRONTING NEGATIVE LABELS

Now it's time to reflect on the labels we've taken on—whether they've come from our own negative self-talk, the hurtful words of others, or stereotypes that have been imposed upon us. These labels, along with the harmful words we often speak over ourselves, can shape how we see our worth. Let's take a moment to recognize them so we can begin the journey of releasing their hold.

Step 1: Identify the Labels
Reflect on the negative labels you've internalized. Take a moment to consider the labels that have come from your own negative self-talk, those given by people who hurt or bullied you, and stereotypes that may have been imposed on you. As you think through this, refer back to the list of examples and identify any that resonate with your experience.

Step 2: Write Down Each Label
List each label on a separate line. Be specific and honest about the labels you have carried.

CONFRONTING NEGATIVE LABELS

Step 3: Reflect on the Impact

For each label, write a few sentences about how it has affected your self-esteem, behavior, and choices. Consider how these labels have shaped your self-perception and interactions with others.

Step 4: Challenge the Labels

Identify any evidence that contradicts each label. Write down positive attributes or achievements that disprove the negative labels.

THE TRUTH OF WHO YOU ARE

Take a break from the activity for a moment.

As you've confronted the negative labels that have shaped how you see yourself, it's important to remember who has the ultimate authority over your identity: God. The world may try to place labels on you—labels from hurtful words, stereotypes, or even your own negative thoughts—but none of those labels have the final say.

God is the One who truly knows you. He is the Creator, the One who formed you with purpose, love, and care. The labels He places on you are the ones that reflect your true worth and identity.

When you align yourself with the truth of who God says you are, the false labels lose their power. God calls you loved, worthy, redeemed, whole, and free. These are the labels that stand unshaken, regardless of what you've been told or how you've felt. Only His voice matters—the One who speaks truth, grace, and love over you.

As you continue this journey of releasing the false labels and embracing the truth, reflect on the fact that God's words over your life carry eternal weight. His authority is greater than any hurt or lie you've believed. When you choose to accept the labels He's given you, you are stepping into the fullness of who He created you to be.

Let this truth sink into your heart: God's labels are the only ones that matter.

They remind you of your worth and your purpose. Trust in His authority over your life, and as you move forward, allow His truth to shape your thoughts, actions, and the way you see yourself.

WHAT LABEL DOES GOD PLACE ON YOU ?

As you release the false labels from your life, it's important to embrace the true identity God has given you. These scriptures reveal the powerful names and roles He has placed on His beloved children—reminders of your worth, purpose, and place in His family. Let these truths sink into your heart and fully embrace the identity God has lovingly spoken over you.

Take a moment to explore how God describes and labels His children.

Children of God - 1 Peter 2:9
"But you are a chosen people, a royal priesthood, a holy nation, a people for God's own possession, so that you may proclaim the excellencies of Him who has called you out of darkness into His marvelous light."

Beloved -1 John 3:1
"See what great love the Father has lavished on us, that we should be called children of God! And that is what we are!"

Friend of God - John 15:15
"I no longer call you servants, because a servant does not know his master's business. Instead, I have called you friends, for everything that I learned from my Father I have made known to you."

Salt and Light of the World - Matthew 5:13-14
"You are the salt of the earth... You are the light of the world."

More than Conquerors- Romans 8:37
"No, in all these things we are more than conquerors through him who loved us."

Forgiven - Ephesians 1:7
"In him we have redemption through his blood, the forgiveness of sins, in accordance with the riches of God's grace"

CONFRONTING NEGATIVE LABELS

Step 5: Letting Go

For each label, write a statement of release, affirming your decision to let go of the negative label. Replace it with what God says about you and a positive affirmation.

Example:

Label: "Unworthy"
Impact: This label has made me doubt my value and hesitate to pursue opportunities.
Contradiction: *"Greater love has no one than this, that a person will lay down his life for his friends."* (John 15:13) Jesus died for me, he believes I am worthy of this sacrifice.
Release Statement: I release the label "unworthy" and affirm that I am valuable and deserving of success. I am a child of God worthy of love and life lived to its fullest.

CONFRONTING NEGATIVE LABELS

Step 5: Letting Go - Continued

EMBRACING YOUR TRUE IDENTITY

Now that you've reflected on the harmful labels you've released and explored the truth of who God says you are, it's time to claim your new identity. The labels the world places on us do not define our worth—God's truth does.

For this activity, take a moment to consider the labels God has spoken over you in the scriptures you've just read. What resonates with you? What identity do you feel called to embrace? This is your opportunity to step into the fullness of who you are in Christ.

Inside the sticker below, write the new labels you are claiming for yourself.

These are the words that represent your true identity in Christ—labels that reflect the love, grace, and purpose God has placed on your life. Be bold, be specific, and embrace the transformation that comes with renewing your mind and claiming the truth of who you are.

HELLO

Chosen. Loved. Known.

You Are God's Child.

PRAY

This guided prayer is an opportunity to release the negative labels you've carried and invite God's healing into those areas of your life. Seek His guidance in letting go of the hurt and accepting the truth of your worth in His eyes. Allow His love and forgiveness to bring peace and renewal to your heart.

Dear Heavenly Father (Abba),

I come before You today, humbled and ready to release the labels I have carried for far too long. These labels, whether placed on me by others, inherited from circumstances beyond my control, or born from my own negative thoughts, have shaped how I've seen myself. They have caused pain, doubt, and separation from the truth of who You say I am.

Lord, I acknowledge that holding onto these labels has kept me in bondage, and I no longer need to carry them. I ask for Your help in forgiving those who have spoken hurtful words over me, for breaking free from labels I was born into, and most importantly, in forgiving myself for believing these lies. Grant me the strength to rebuke the worldly labels and release each one, replacing them with the truth of Your love and grace.

As I let go, let Your voice be louder and truer than any other. Fill my heart with Your peace, and remind me that my identity is found in You alone—not in the words, actions, or judgments of others. Help me to walk in the truth of who I am—a beloved child of God, worthy of love and acceptance. Guide me to see myself through Your eyes, and to live in the freedom that comes from embracing the identity You have given me.

Thank You for Your forgiveness, Your healing, and the new identity You offer me in Christ. I place my trust in You as I continue on this journey of healing, knowing that You are always with me, leading me toward wholeness and peace.

In Jesus' name, Amen.

REFLECT

As you reflect on the labels you've carried, take a moment to acknowledge the weight they've had on your heart and mind.

These labels—born from negative self-talk, the words of others, or societal stereotypes—have shaped how you see yourself and influenced your decisions. But today, you've begun the powerful process of letting go, making room for the truth of who you are in Christ.

Forgiveness plays a vital role in this journey. By forgiving those who have spoken harmful words over you and yourself for believing them, you open the door to healing.

Rebuke the lies that have shaped your identity, allowing the new, God-given labels—**Loved, Worthy, Redeemed, Whole**—to take root.

Consider how your perspective might shift if you chose to embrace these truths instead of the labels that once held you captive. Remember, you are co-authoring your life with God. Invite Him into this process and allow His guidance to shape your narrative.

Change doesn't happen overnight, and healing takes time. Be patient and kind with yourself as you work through this. Every step you take, no matter how small, is progress. Trust that as you continue this journey, God will lead you toward deeper healing and freedom.

SECTION 8

The Path to Forgiveness of Self

This section explores the transformative journey of accepting forgiveness for yourself. Through reflective journaling exercises, meaningful scriptures, and prayers, you'll discover how to embrace self-compassion and release the burdens of guilt and regret. You'll also learn the impact of withholding forgiveness from yourself, and how to share your grief with God.

With guidance from biblical teachings on rest, renewal, and peace, this section provides practical steps to help you find freedom and healing through the grace of forgiveness of self.

THE JOURNEY TOWARD FORGIVENESS OF SELF

Accepting forgiveness for yourself is a crucial yet often challenging aspect of personal growth and well-being. Holding onto guilt, shame, and self-blame for past mistakes creates a heavy burden that hinders our ability to move forward and lead fulfilling lives. As Christians, we find comfort in the understanding that God offers forgiveness to all through Jesus' sacrifice. By accepting this gift of grace, we can begin to extend the same forgiveness to ourselves.

This transformative process requires patience, self-compassion, and commitment. Meditating on scriptures that emphasize God's love, mercy, and forgiveness—such as Ephesians 4:32 or 1 John 1:9—can help ground your journey. **Reflect on how God's forgiveness serves as a foundation for your own journey toward forgiveness of self.**

Remember, accepting forgiveness for yourself is an ongoing process where progress matters more than perfection. As you cultivate self-compassion and engage in practical steps to forgive yourself, you will unlock the path to healing and growth. With time, you'll develop greater resilience and self-understanding, allowing the ability to extend forgiveness to others to become a more natural occurrence as you grow in empathy and understanding for yourself and your choices.

Love yourself!

A PRAYER FOR GUIDANCE

Take a moment to write a heartfelt prayer or letter to God. Express your gratitude for His forgiveness and ask for His guidance and strength as you continue on the journey of forgiving yourself.

THE POWER OF SELF-FORGIVENESS

In our journey of spiritual growth and emotional healing, we often focus on forgiving others but overlook the critical practice of forgiving ourselves. This oversight can lead to prolonged shame and emotional distress. Self-forgiveness acts as the rudder of our lives, guiding us toward healthier relationships.

Don't Fall for the Shame Trap

Holding onto shame for past actions—whether done in ignorance or with full knowledge—creates barriers in our relationships. When we refuse God's forgiveness, we are essentially playing God, denying His grace over our lives.

The Consequences of Unforgiveness

Failure to forgive oneself can lead to spiritual disconnection, mental health issues like anxiety and depression, and low self-esteem. Without self-forgiveness, we risk becoming trapped in negativity that hinders our growth.

Use God's Forgiveness as a Model

Scripture emphasizes God's willingness to forgive, providing a model for how we should treat ourselves. By embracing the truth of His forgiveness, we can mirror this compassion in our self-perception.

Enjoy the Freedom of Self-Forgiveness

Embracing self-forgiveness opens the door to spiritual renewal and emotional healing. It is time to release shame and accept God's grace, allowing self-compassion to transform your life.

God wants this for you!

THE IMPACT OF NOT FORGIVING YOURSELF

Research has shown that individuals who struggle with forgiving themselves are more likely to experience negative emotional states, such as depression, anxiety, and shame. They may also engage in maladaptive coping mechanisms, such as substance abuse, self-harm, or avoidance behaviors.

Reflect on how holding onto self-blame has affected your life and relationships.

Self-forgiveness has only recently begun to be studied systematically, and there is still a paucity of empirical research on the tendency to self-forgive. Hall and Fincham (2005) argue that there are three essential steps to self-forgiveness.

First, one must acknowledge the commission of a transgression against the self and accept responsibility for that transgression. One must then experience feelings of guilt and regret.

Finally, one must overcome these feelings (i.e., accepting forgiveness for oneself), and in doing so, experience a motivational change away from self-punishment towards self-acceptance.

For example, Wohl, DeShea, and Wahkinney (2008), showed that for people who experienced the unwanted end to a romantic relationship, increases in self-blame predicted increases in depressive affect. This effect was mediated by self-forgiveness. As self-forgiveness is a positive self-referent attitudinal shift, self-forgiveness undermined negative feelings toward the self.

When we live by this spiritual discipline of accepting and forgiving ourselves allows us to more fully live obedience in the second most important commandment, which is to **Love our Neighbors as Ourselves!**

SCRIPTURES TO EMBRACE FORGIVENESS OF SELF

Releasing Shame and Accepting Grace

Luke 23:34
"But Jesus was saying, 'Father, forgive them; for they do not know what they are doing.'"

1 Timothy 1:13
"Even though I was formerly a blasphemer and a persecutor and a violent aggressor. Yet I was shown mercy because I acted ignorantly in unbelief."

Luke 12:47-48
"And that slave who knew his master's will and did not get ready or act in accord with his will, will receive many lashes, but the one who did not know it, and committed deeds worthy of a flogging, will receive but few."

The Importance of Accepting Forgiveness For Yourself

1 John 1:9
"If we confess our sins, He is faithful and righteous, so that He will forgive us our sins and cleanse us from all unrighteousness."

Psalm 103:12
"As far as the east is from the west, so far has He removed our transgressions from us."

Freedom Through Forgiveness of Self

Colossians 3:13
"Bear with each other and forgive one another if any of you has a grievance against someone. Forgive as the Lord forgave you."

PRACTICE FORGIVENESS OF SELF

To identify areas where you're holding onto shame, accept God's forgiveness, and practice accepting forgiveness for yourself.

Step 1: Identify an Instance of Shame, Regret or Self Condemnation

List 3-5 past actions or decisions that you're still holding onto shame about. For each, write down:

a) What happened
b) Why you feel ashamed
c) How this shame is affecting your life now

PRACTICE FORGIVENESS OF SELF

Step 2: List the Consequences

List the negative consequences you have experienced as a result of not forgiving yourself. Consider how these consequences have impacted your mental health, relationships, and overall well-being. Then bring it to God.

Step 3: Acknowledge God's Forgiveness

For each item on your list, write out or meditate on this truth: "God has forgiven me for this through Jesus Christ." (*You might find it helpful to write out 1 John 1:9 personalized to your situation.*)

PRACTICE FORGIVENESS OF SELF

Step 4: Release the Shame

For each item, write a statement accepting forgiveness for yourself. For example: "As I am already forgiven, I forgive myself for [action]. I choose to release this and accept God's forgiveness and love."

Step 5: Positive Affirmation

Write a positive affirmation or truth to counter each shame-based thought. For example, if you feel "I am unworthy." your affirmation might be "I am worthy of love and belonging because God loves me unconditionally. Only God's truth can cut through the shame and lies to bring me into wholeness."

PRACTICE FORGIVENESS OF SELF

Step 6: Moving Forward

In Romans 8:28, we are reminded of God's promise: 'And we know that God causes all things to work together for good to those who love God, to those who are called according to His purpose.'

Reflect on how He has transformed a challenge or hardship in your life for good. What lesson did you learn through this experience? Write down one or two ways you can use this insight to grow personally and to support others on their journey.

PRACTICE FORGIVENESS OF SELF

Step 7: Reinforce and Embrace
Choose a relevant Bible verse to meditate on daily for the next week. This will help reinforce your decision to embrace forgiveness of self.

_____
_____
_____
_____
_____
_____
_____
_____
_____

Remember, accepting forgiveness for yourself is a process. It will take time and repeated effort to fully release shame and embrace God's forgiveness. Be patient with yourself. As you practice accepting forgiveness for yourself, you'll likely experience greater peace, improved relationships, and a closer connection with God.

By accepting forgiveness — both from God and yourself — you open the door to healing and growth. You free yourself from the burden of shame and create space for positive experiences and deeper spiritual connection.

> Remember, you are worthy of forgiveness and love, not because of what you do or don't do, but because of who you are: **a beloved child of God.**

PRAY

Let this guided prayer help solidify the work you've begun, as you release the burdens of the past and fully accept the forgiveness God has already granted you. Take this moment to align your heart with His grace and embrace the freedom that comes with letting go.

Dear Heavenly Father (Abba),

I come before You, acknowledging that I've been holding onto guilt and shame for far too long. In not accepting Your forgiveness, I've been playing God by holding onto unforgiveness toward myself, as though I knew what I deserved. Now, I recognize that it is Your grace and mercy alone that set me free.

Lord, I understand now that forgiveness of self is the rudder of my life, steering me toward the peace and healing You have promised. Without it, I am adrift in a sea of regret, unable to move forward. But You, in Your mercy, have already forgiven me, and now it's time for me to forgive myself.

Help me to release the heavy burdens I've placed upon my heart. Teach me to let go of the self-blame and guilt that I have allowed to linger, and instead, to fully embrace the forgiveness and love You offer. Remind me that in holding onto shame, I am not walking in the truth of who You say I am.

Father, guide me to stop playing God over my own life, and to surrender my need for control. Fill me with Your peace, and lead me in the freedom that comes from forgiving myself as You have already forgiven me.

Thank You for Your endless grace, for the new beginning You offer, and for the strength to accept it. I trust You to lead me on this journey toward healing and wholeness.

In Jesus' name, Amen.

REFLECT

As you reflect on the exercises you've just completed, take a moment to acknowledge the progress you've made.

God's forgiveness has already been granted—the next step is for you to fully accept it and recognize your worthiness of His grace. Guilt, shame, and self-blame no longer have a place in your heart or mind.

This journey is about more than releasing old labels; it is about reclaiming your identity as a beloved child of God.

Before moving on to the next section, please return to Section 4: "Starting the Forgiveness Journey" where you previously selected someone from your forgiveness inventory to work through.

This time, turn the lens of forgiveness inward. Apply the same exercises and principles you used to forgive others, but now for yourself. (Additional activity sheets can be found in the back of the workbook, and you are encouraged to make copies for your personal use.)

God's forgiveness has already been extended to you; now is the time to fully embrace that truth and experience the freedom it brings. Let go of the weight of the past, and step into the lightness and joy that comes with accepting His grace. Allow His love to guide you on this journey of healing, drawing you closer to spiritual and emotional wholeness with each step you take.

Remember, you are never walking this path alone—God is with you, guiding and supporting you every step of the way.

SECTION 9

Walking in Long Suffering

In this section, you'll uncover the meaning of long suffering and its essential role in the forgiveness process.

Through personal testimony and scripture, you'll explore how enduring difficult times with faith can transform your journey of healing. An engaging activity will help you reflect on your own experiences of long suffering, while biblical insights on love, patience, and hope guide you toward a deeper understanding of God's presence during seasons of hardship.

UNDERSTANDING THE CONCEPT OF LONG-SUFFERING

Long-suffering is a deeply profound and often misunderstood experience, one that can only be fully grasped through personal trials. It's more than just enduring difficulty; **it's about a patient, steadfast love that chooses to persist through pain, misunderstanding, and even injustice.** When you seek the heart of Jesus and ask to love others as He loves, long-suffering becomes a tangible part of your journey. It is through this experience that you **draw nearer to Jesus, gaining a deeper understanding of the sacrifice He made and the endurance of His love for us.**

Jesus exemplified long-suffering through His life, particularly in how He continued to love humanity despite the rejection, betrayal, and suffering He endured. By embracing this aspect of Christ's love, we are invited to feel a glimpse of what He experienced for us. Through long-suffering, we can begin to comprehend the **depth of His sacrifice and the boundless nature of His grace.**

This kind of love transforms the heart. It is a love that chooses forgiveness over resentment, patience over anger, and faith over doubt. Long-suffering is a path of growth, not one of weakness or passivity. It teaches us to love others with a heart like Jesus, even when it's hard, painful, or unfair. It also shows us **how intimately connected we are to God's divine plan when we endure suffering with love and grace.**

To truly understand the heart of Jesus, we must embrace long-suffering. It is through these moments of enduring love that we grow closer to Him and gain a deeper understanding of His limitless love for us. This concept may feel overwhelming at first, but **when we choose to walk in long-suffering, we are choosing to love like Christ**, who never gave up on us despite His suffering.

A TESTIMONY OF LONG-SUFFERING

Today, as I sat with my husband, I learned about long-suffering by choosing to love him repeatedly, regardless of my thoughts, opinions, or his actions. This choice to forgive him required me to ensure my list was complete, leaving nothing behind that could fester and cause a rift in our relationship later on. As I reflected on these areas, I thought about the pain in my heart from not being able to be with my mom these past couple of weeks due to circumstances. I considered all the credit I wanted for myself, and as I gathered my list of righteous things I thought I would still forgive him for, I could hear Jesus chuckle, saying, "It's almost like long-suffering."

I realized I had never felt long-suffering before, and Jesus explained that it is usually felt the most when you have children. As I didn't have children, my closest relationship was with my husband. Had I not experienced some long-suffering in the early stages of my marriage, I would not have known the pain, sacrifice, longing, sadness, hope, trust, and faith that are all intertwined in this concept. I genuinely laughed with Jesus as I prayed, thanking Him for loving me so much and wanting to reveal His heart and love to me. He allowed me to feel what He felt for me, even though I was just getting a glimpse of it with my husband, while Jesus has spent a lifetime loving and long suffering for me.

This is why it is wise to look at the gifts we received in the offenses against us, and although it might not sound fair or fun, it is the closest I could grasp the meaning of the phrase "transformation of the mind." When I think about that, I realize that I truly desire a transformation of my mind, to have my mind in sync with the Creator of the universe, the beginning and the end, the very Word that brought us into existence.

Your Fellow Warrior and Journeyman,

Kat

CONNECTING WITH LONG-SUFFERING IN YOUR JOURNEY

Long-suffering doesn't just shape our relationships with others; it also transforms our relationship with God. It deepens our faith, builds endurance, and ultimately aligns our hearts with the eternal love and patience that Jesus has for each of us. As we experience long-suffering, we are being shaped into His likeness, and our ability to love grows stronger with each challenge.

As you explore the concept of long-suffering, consider these reflective questions to help deepen your understanding and apply this lesson to your own experiences.

Think about a time when you've had to endure a difficult situation with patience and love. How did that experience shape your heart and your relationship with others?

_____
_____
_____

In what ways can you invite Jesus to help you practice long-suffering in your current relationships, especially when it's hard to forgive or be patient?

_____
_____
_____

How has embracing the concept of long-suffering deepened your faith and brought you closer to understanding the love Christ has for you?

_____
_____
_____

SCRIPTURES ON LOVE, LONG-SUFFERING, AND HOPE

Love and long-suffering are deeply intertwined, as true love requires patience, perseverance, and endurance through difficulties. The following verses show how love, guided by the Holy Spirit, sustains us through trials and suffering, ultimately building character and hope. In embracing long-suffering, we reflect the depth of Christ's love and find strength in the midst of hardship.

1 Corinthians 13:4-7

"Love is patient, love is kind. It does not envy, it does not boast, it is not proud. It does not dishonor others, it is not self-seeking, it is not easily angered, it keeps no record of wrongs. Love does not delight in evil but rejoices with the truth. It always protects, always trusts, always hopes, always perseveres."

Galatians 5:22-23

"But the fruit of the Spirit is love, joy, peace, long-suffering, kindness, goodness, faithfulness, gentleness, self-control. Against such, there is no law."

Romans 5:3-5

"Not only so, but we also glory in our sufferings, because we know that suffering produces perseverance; perseverance, character; and character, hope. And hope does not put us to shame, because God's love has been poured out into our hearts through the Holy Spirit, who has been given to us."

PRAY

Pause for a moment and invite God into this space, as you prepare your heart for prayer. Let His presence bring comfort and strength as you seek His guidance through your season of long suffering.

Dear Heavenly Father (Abba),

In moments of hardship, when the weight of my struggles feels heavy, I come before You with an open heart. I thank You for being present with me, even in my times of deepest sorrow and uncertainty. You are the God who sees me, who knows my pain, and who walks with me through every trial.

Lord, I confess that enduring long seasons of suffering is not easy, but I trust that You are using these trials to shape me and grow my faith. Help me to remain patient when my heart is weary and my soul feels burdened. Teach me to surrender my pain and struggles to You, knowing that Your plans are higher than my understanding. Give me the strength to persevere, even when the path seems long and the end distant.

Grant me the grace to lean on You in my weakest moments, to trust in Your timing, and to find peace in the knowledge that You are working all things for my good. Lord, in this season of waiting, help me to find hope in Your promises and to rest in Your love.

As I endure these trials, fill my heart with compassion and patience. Let me grow in wisdom and resilience, knowing that my suffering is not in vain but is producing in me a deeper faith and reliance on You.

In Jesus' name, Amen.

REFLECT

Take a moment to reflect on the journey of long suffering and the grace that comes through enduring difficult seasons with faith.

Long suffering is not a passive experience but a profound, active expression of trust in God. It is through these times that our hearts are refined, and our reliance on Him deepens.

Consider how God has walked with you through seasons of hardship. Even when the road feels long and the burden heavy, He promises to never leave your side.

His love is unwavering, and His strength is made perfect in our weakness.

How has enduring through challenges shaped your heart and spirit? Reflect on the ways in which your faith has been stretched, and where God's peace has sustained you.

Think about the fruit that long suffering has produced in your life—patience, resilience, compassion, and a greater understanding of God's sustaining grace.

As you move forward, trust that God's timing is perfect, and that He is using this season for your growth and His glory. Let this reflection remind you that long suffering is not in vain; it is a journey of transformation, drawing you closer to the heart of God.

Let His strength be your guide as you continue to press on in faith, knowing that with Him, there is always hope.

SECTION 10

The Forgiveness Jellyfish

This section introduces the Forgiveness Jellyfish, a powerful visual tool for understanding how a single event (the head) can have multiple layers of trauma and unforgiveness (the tentacles) attached to it. You will explore how different people or circumstances may have contributed to the pain stemming from one core event.

With an example provided for guidance, you'll engage in an activity to map out your own Situational Jellyfish, identifying areas that need healing. The section concludes with a focus on addressing and healing each of these "tentacles" of offense as part of your forgiveness journey.

INTRODUCING THE FORGIVENESS JELLYFISH

Forgiveness can often feel overwhelming when a single offense or difficult event has far-reaching consequences, impacting many areas of your life.

This is where the "Forgiveness Jellyfish" exercise comes in.

It's a tool to help you visually identify and address the multiple layers of hurt, pain, and consequences stemming from a single, central offense or event that requires forgiveness.

Think of a jellyfish: its body represents the main event or offense, while its tentacles symbolize the ripple effects—those additional hurts, issues, and consequences that radiate out from the central experience. These tentacles can stretch into many different areas of your life, often without you fully realizing the extent of their reach.

The purpose of this exercise is to give you a comprehensive understanding of how one event can affect multiple aspects of your life. It's easy to focus solely on the main incident, like a divorce, illness, abuse, or career setback, but we often overlook the tentacles—**the associated pain and consequences that are just as important to recognize and address.** These tentacles can be people, actions, inactions, or emotional responses tied to the central offense/event.

ADDRESSING THE TENTACLES OF OFFENSE

Offenses are often complex and layered. When we don't address all the connected aspects—the tentacles—we risk leaving unresolved pain buried beneath the surface. This can lead to ongoing emotional or spiritual issues. The goal of the situational jellyfish exercise is to bring these hidden areas into the light, to recognize the full scope of what needs healing and forgiveness, not just the main event itself.

By mapping out the central offense/event and each of its tentacles, you create a more complete picture of the situation. You can visually see how far-reaching the trauma is and how different people or circumstances played a role in your experience. This exercise helps you understand that forgiveness isn't just about the core event—**it's about addressing the ripple effects as well.**

Once you've identified the tentacles, **the next step is to bring them before God for healing and forgiveness.** You can release these hurts and consequences one by one, seeking to let go of each painful connection tied to the central event. Forgiveness, in this sense, becomes a multi-layered process that requires patience, honesty, and a willingness to acknowledge all the pieces of the puzzle.

In summary, the Forgiveness Jellyfish exercise helps you:

- Identify the central offense (the jellyfish's body) and its far-reaching effects (the tentacles).

- Bring to light every connected hurt, consequence, or unresolved issue.

- Systematically work through forgiveness and healing with God's guidance.

SITUATIONAL JELLYFISH IN ACTION

Now that we've introduced the concept of the Forgiveness Jellyfish, this page will take a deeper look at how unresolved hurt can manifest through a specific example.

Every offense is unique, and just like a jellyfish has a varying number of tentacles, the ripple effects of the event can extend in different ways depending on the situation. This example explores how multiple tentacles—such as betrayal, inaction, self-blame, and more—can all be interconnected, revealing the full scope of what needs healing.

As you follow along, keep in mind that each person's experience will have its own distinct set of tentacles, each deserving attention and care in the process of forgiveness and healing.

In this example, we will be exploring the experience of someone who endured childhood sexual abuse.

The Body of the Jellyfish
The central offense—the jellyfish's body—is the sexual abuse itself. This is the core event, the primary source of hurt. However, like the many tentacles of a jellyfish, this single event has multiple ripple effects that extend into various areas of the person's life, each representing a different person or institution related to the offense that needs to be addressed.

Tentacle 1: Inaction of Family Members
One tentacle could represent the inaction of family member(s) who may have been aware of the abuse but failed to protect the individual or take necessary action. The hurt here isn't just the abuse, but the feelings of abandonment or betrayal that arise when those who should have protected you remained silent or indifferent. This inaction creates an additional layer of pain that lingers, often unaddressed.

SITUATIONAL JELLYFISH IN ACTION

Tentacle 2: Betrayal and Trust Issues
Another tentacle could symbolize the deep sense of betrayal that develops from being harmed by a person or institution you trusted. This betrayal can create long-lasting issues with trust, making it difficult to form healthy relationships in the future. The pain caused by broken trust extends beyond the abuser—it can affect how the person interacts with others for years to come.

Tentacle 3: Punishment or Dismissal for Speaking Up
A different tentacle could represent the dismissal or even punishment the individual faced when trying to speak up about the abuse. Maybe they weren't believed, or their disclosure was minimized or ignored. The person might have been told to keep quiet or was blamed for causing trouble. This can lead to a fear of speaking out in future situations and feelings of helplessness.

Tentacle 4: Self-Blame and Shame
A particularly painful tentacle could represent the self-blame or shame that many survivors carry. They may internalize the abuse, believing it was somehow their fault, or they may feel ashamed of what happened, even though it was completely beyond their control. This tentacle often runs deep, affecting their sense of self-worth and identity, possibly leading to patterns of self-punishment or self-sabotage.

Tentacle 5: Emotional Numbness or Avoidance
Another possible tentacle is emotional numbness or avoidance, where the person shuts down emotionally to protect themselves from the pain of the trauma. They may avoid difficult conversations, situations, or relationships that could trigger memories of the abuse. This avoidance might bring temporary relief, but in the long run, it prevents emotional healing and leaves the underlying pain unresolved.

FORGIVENESS JELLYFISH IN ACTION

Tentacle 6: Impact on Future Relationships
A tentacle could also symbolize the impact on future relationships. For example, the person may struggle to form healthy, trusting connections with others. They may find themselves repeating unhealthy patterns in relationships or avoiding intimacy altogether out of fear of being hurt again.

Tentacle 7: Effects on Mental Health
Finally, another tentacle could represent the mental health effects of the trauma, such as anxiety, depression, or post-traumatic stress. These are often direct consequences of the abuse and can persist for years if not properly addressed.

By identifying each of these tentacles, the person is able to bring all the interconnected pieces of their trauma into the light. What was once hidden or left unaddressed can now be seen with clarity, allowing the process of healing to begin. While the abuse is the central offense, the additional hurts—inaction, betrayal, punishment, self-blame, emotional avoidance, and mental health challenges—are just as important to acknowledge and work through.

Each tentacle represents an area that has carried its own weight of pain, and each requires attention and care.

FORGIVENESS JELLYFISH IN ACTION

Before you begin creating your own forgiveness jellyfish, take a moment to prepare yourself for what can be an emotional process.

As you reflect on the central offense and the ripple effects it has had on your life, remember that this exercise is about bringing everything to the surface—every pain, every hurt. Take your time as you identify and map out each of the "tentacles" extending from the core event. **There's no limit to how many tentacles you can add; each one represents an important part of your experience.** Allow yourself the space to process, and be gentle with yourself as you work through these deeply personal aspects of your journey.

Keep in mind that you may need to revisit this process for multiple experiences in your life. Each traumatic event might represent a different jellyfish, with its own set of tentacles extending into various areas of your life. Take your time with each one, and as needed, create additional jellyfish for different events to fully explore and map out all the connected pain and consequences.

When you're ready, begin by identifying the central offense as the body of your jellyfish, and from there, add each tentacle as it comes to mind, representing the connected hurts and consequences as well as the people and institutions that correlate.

This process can be returned to whenever you're ready to face new aspects of your journey, recognizing that healing is a layered and ongoing process.

CREATE YOUR FORGIVENESS JELLYFISH

CREATE YOUR FORGIVENESS JELLYFISH

CREATE YOUR FORGIVENESS JELLYFISH

CREATE YOUR FORGIVENESS JELLYFISH

CREATE YOUR FORGIVENESS JELLYFISH

HEALING THE TENTACLES OF OFFENSE

Now that you've brought these hidden aspects of your unresolved hurt to the surface, it's essential to remember that God is present, ready to guide and offer His healing for every layer you've uncovered.

By visualizing the tentacles of offense, the people and institutions connected to this hurt, and bringing them before God, you have invited His grace into every part of your journey. **Forgiveness becomes more than a single act—it's a multi-layered process of releasing the hurts tied to each tentacle.** Each step, each moment of surrender, allows God's love to work through the pain. With His guidance, you can release the trauma, offering each part to Him for healing and peace.

God calls us to forgive not only for the sake of others but for our own freedom. As you work through each tentacle, **you're not only forgiving others for their roles but also freeing yourself from the burden of the past.** Through prayer and faith, God provides the strength to heal every layer of the trauma, leading to emotional, spiritual, and mental freedom. This process is a partnership with God, trusting that He can bring wholeness where there was once hurt.

To move forward, **take an inventory of the people and institutions connected to the central offense**—the tentacles extending from the body. Identify each source of pain and reflect on how it has impacted your life.

Now, with this inventory, it is time to revisit Section 4. For each person or institution identified, use these exercises to systematically bring each piece before God, letting go of the pain one step at a time.

By releasing these areas to God, you invite His healing and allow forgiveness to transform your heart and mind.

PRAY

Take a moment to quiet your heart and reflect on what you've uncovered through the forgiveness jellyfish activity—let this guided prayer help you release those burdens into God's loving hands.

Dear Heavenly Father (Abba),

I come before You with a heart that is weary from carrying the weight of so many hurts and burdens. As I have drawn out the areas of pain and struggle from my past, I see now how deeply connected these experiences are to my heart and soul. Each "tentacle" of this offense has affected me in ways I didn't fully realize, but I know that none of this is hidden from You.

I surrender each of these hurts to You now, trusting that You are the healer of my heart. You see every wound, every memory, and every scar. I ask that Your grace would begin to flow into each part of my story, gently restoring and renewing the broken pieces within me.

Where I have felt anger, bitterness, or fear, bring Your peace. Where I have carried guilt or shame, cover me with Your love and forgiveness. Help me to let go of the things I've been holding onto, so I may walk in the freedom You offer.

I ask for Your strength to forgive—not just those who have hurt me, but also myself, for holding onto this pain for so long. Fill me with the courage to release what I cannot control, and the wisdom to trust in Your perfect timing and plan for healing.

Abba, remind me that I am not alone in this journey. Just as You have been with me through the difficult times, I know You are here now, guiding me as I walk this path of forgiveness. Help me to move forward with grace, trusting that You are transforming my heart, just as You promise to make all things new.

Thank You for carrying me when I have felt weak, and for being my constant source of comfort. I place my past, present, and future in Your hands, knowing that Your love will bring healing and restoration in Your perfect way.

In Jesus' name, Amen.

REFLECT

As you reflect on this prayer and the work you've done in identifying the various areas of hurt in your life, take a moment to recognize how far you've come in this journey.

The process of acknowledging deep wounds can be difficult, but it is a necessary step toward healing. Each person or institution you've identified is a piece of your story that God is ready to transform.

Consider how bringing these hurts to God, layer by layer, is opening the door to His healing and grace. Releasing these burdens, whether from past trauma, personal failures, or ongoing struggles, is an act of trust—trusting that God is not only able to carry the weight but also to heal every wound.

Remember, healing doesn't happen all at once.

Healing is a journey, and each time you return to God with a new layer of pain, you are taking a step closer to freedom. Trust in His timing, and allow His love to guide you as you continue to work through the tentacles of hurt, one by one.

Take this time to reflect on any new thoughts or feelings that have surfaced, and invite God's grace into these areas. How has this process of reflection opened your heart to forgiveness—both of others and of yourself? How might God be using this to shape your journey forward?

SECTION 11

Uncovering Hidden Hurt

In this section, you will embark on a timeline activity to explore the hidden hurts and unforgiveness that may still be lingering in your life. By reflecting on different stages and events, you'll uncover deeply buried emotions and memories. This process, though it may stir up old pain, is a crucial step on the path toward healing and freedom.

Afterward, you'll be encouraged to process these feelings, recognizing that each step forward, no matter how small, brings you closer to emotional and spiritual freedom. The section concludes with a prayer and reflection to ground you in God's peace as you continue this transformative journey.

FACING WHAT IS BURIED WITHIN

In the journey toward forgiveness, one of the hardest steps is recognizing the hurt that lies beneath the surface. **Often, these wounds are not immediately visible, becoming so entangled with our lives that we may not even notice their ongoing impact.** But God invites us to bring these hidden pains into the light, offering us the chance to heal and grow.

> Psalm 139:23-24 says, *"Search me, O God, and know my heart; try me and know my anxious thoughts; and see if there be any hurtful way in me, and lead me in the everlasting way."*

This scripture reminds us that God knows our deepest wounds—even those we've buried—and He desires to lead us into healing. By inviting God into these broken places, we allow His grace to begin the work of restoration.

Though the process of uncovering hidden hurts can be difficult, it is essential to our journey toward peace. **When we bring our pain to God, we open the door to His healing touch.**

> Isaiah 61:1 affirms His promise: *"The Spirit of the Lord God is upon me, because the Lord has anointed me to bring good news to the afflicted; He has sent me to bind up the brokenhearted, to proclaim liberty to captives and freedom to prisoners."*

Just as He mends the brokenhearted, God longs to set you free from the hidden hurts that keep you bound.

Take a moment to ask God to search your heart, revealing what has been hidden. **As you move forward in this journey, trust that God is with you, ready to guide you with His compassion and strength.** Each step you take is a step closer to true healing and peace.

UNCOVERING HIDDEN HURT AND UNFORGIVENESS

Sometimes, hidden hurts from our past linger unseen, quietly affecting our emotions, relationships, and peace. This activity helps uncover these buried feelings and guides you in letting them go.

By creating a historical timeline, you'll be able to map out different stages of your life and reflect on events that may still carry emotional weight. This exercise will help you identify areas where unforgiveness might be lingering and guide you in working toward healing and freedom.

Step 1: Identify Significant Life Stages

Start by listing major periods in your life. Think of distinct phases such as childhood, high school, college, work, or different relationships. These stages will help you organize your reflections. If you experienced challenges like being bullied at school, work, or home, consider these as potential starting points. Write them out below.

UNCOVERING HIDDEN HURT AND UNFORGIVENESS

Step 2: Choose One Life Stage and Map a Timeline

From the life stages you've listed, choose one that feels particularly significant or unresolved. Create a timeline for this stage, focusing on the sequence of events. Start by mapping what led up to the experience, the key events that defined it, and what happened afterward. This will help you uncover patterns and the ripple effects of that time in your life, allowing you to better understand how this specific stage shaped your emotional journey.

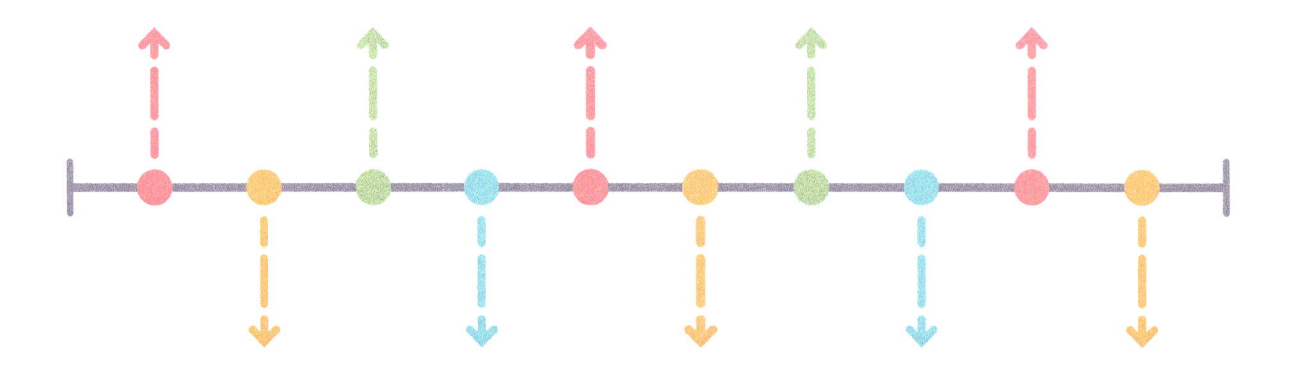

UNCOVERING HIDDEN HURT AND UNFORGIVENESS

Step 3: Reflect on the Positive and Negative Aspects

Take time to reflect on the key moments that stand out. Consider both the positive and negative aspects of this stage, focusing on the events that had the most emotional impact. Identify which experiences brought growth and joy, and which left emotional scars. Remember that events do not cause emotional scars; people do. This reflection will help you gain a deeper understanding of how this period influenced your personal and spiritual development.

UNCOVERING HIDDEN HURT AND UNFORGIVENESS

Step 4: Note Down Painful Experiences

As you reflect on this specific life stage, take note of any painful or challenging experiences that stand out. This could include moments of betrayal, unfair treatment, personal disappointments, or times when you felt deeply hurt. The goal is to pinpoint the events that left lasting emotional wounds, helping you recognize the areas in need of healing from Jesus.

UNCOVERING HIDDEN HURT AND UNFORGIVENESS

Step 5: Assess Your Emotional Response

For each experience you've listed, think about how it makes you feel now. Do you still feel anger, resentment, or hurt when you remember these events? Write these feelings down. This step will help you gauge your current emotional response and identify lingering pain.

Step 6: Identify Areas of Unforgiveness

If any of the experiences still stir up strong negative emotions, it may indicate that there's lingering unforgiveness. Identify both people and events tied to these unresolved feelings. Write them down below.

UNCOVERING HIDDEN HURT AND UNFORGIVENESS

Step 7: Look for Lessons and Blessings

Part of the forgiveness process is recognizing the lessons and blessings that may have come out of difficult times. Even in the midst of hardship, there can be moments of growth, wisdom, or unexpected blessings. Reflect on how these painful experiences have shaped you and what you may have learned. Keep a note of these for future moments of gratitude.

_____
_____
_____
_____
_____
_____
_____
_____

Step 8: Revisit and Expand Your Journey

At your own pace, return to the list of significant life stages you originally created. Take the time to work through this entire exercise for each stage that you feel may hold hidden hurt or unresolved unforgiveness. Healing is a process, and as you grow, new insights may emerge. Regularly review your progress, update your timeline, and prioritize forgiving both others and yourself as you uncover these areas. This ongoing reflection will help you continue releasing burdens and moving forward with emotional and spiritual freedom.

A JOURNEY TOWARD FREEDOM AND HEALING

Each step you've taken to uncover past hurts is a step toward God's light, where His healing awaits. The journey may not feel easy, but remember that God is near, comforting you as you let go of the weight you've carried for so long.

Psalm 147:3
"He heals the brokenhearted and binds up their wounds."

These words remind us that God's heart is tender toward our pain, and He is actively binding up each hurt we bring before Him. Trust that His presence is already at work, stitching together wholeness where there was once brokenness.

When we choose forgiveness, we are choosing to surrender the heavy burdens we have held. Jesus calls us to bring our weariness to Him, promising rest and peace.

Matthew 11:28
"Come to Me, all who are weary and heavy-laden, and I will give you rest."

In this exchange, we let go of bitterness and invite His peace to fill us—a peace that surpasses understanding, guarding our hearts and minds in Christ Jesus.

You are not alone on this path. With each act of surrender, you are stepping closer to the peace and freedom that God has prepared for you.

Let His love and grace be your constant companions, guiding you as you walk in the light of His healing.

PRAY

As you reflect on the hidden hurts in your heart, open yourself to God's presence. Allow this time of prayer to invite His healing into those places, trusting Him to gently uncover what needs to be released.

Dear Heavenly Father (Abba),

I come before You with an open heart, seeking Your healing touch for the wounds I may have hidden away. Lord, You see the pain I've carried—whether I've acknowledged it or not. You know the depths of my heart, the places where hurt has taken root, and I ask You to gently bring those hidden hurts to the surface.

Help me, Father, to face the areas of unforgiveness I may not even realize I've held onto. Give me the courage to name the pain and release it into Your hands. I know that holding onto these hurts only creates barriers between me and the peace You desire for me. So, today, I lay them down before You, trusting that Your love is enough to heal even the deepest wounds.

Lord, teach me to forgive—fully and freely—as You have forgiven me. Show me how to let go of bitterness, resentment, and anger. Where I struggle to forgive, fill my heart with Your grace. Transform my pain into peace, my sorrow into joy, and my bitterness into love.

Thank You for never leaving me, even in my most broken places. Help me to trust in Your perfect timing, knowing that You are at work in my life, bringing healing and restoration. I surrender my heart to You, asking for the strength to forgive, to heal, and to be free.

In Jesus' name, Amen.

REFLECT

Take a moment to sit with what has been revealed during your prayer and reflection.

When we invite God into the hidden places of our heart, He brings to light the hurts we have held on to—sometimes for far longer than we realize. Though this process may feel vulnerable, remember that it is also a journey toward freedom.

Consider the emotions and memories that surfaced. Were there areas you were surprised to revisit? How did God's presence feel as you laid these hurts before Him?

Each step in uncovering these hidden wounds allows God to work His healing power in ways you may not yet see, but trust that He is faithful to complete the work He has begun in you.

Healing is not always instant, but it is always ongoing.

In your exploration, you identified areas of lingering unforgiveness and made an inventory of both people and events tied to these unresolved feelings.

For each person or institution identified, use the individual forgiveness worksheets to systematically bring your pain before God.

For each event on your inventory, explore the deeper emotional impact using the Forgiveness Jellyfish exercise.

SECTION 12

The Gifts of Forgiveness

In this section, you'll delve into the spiritual and emotional rewards that forgiveness brings. By exploring scripture, you will uncover the powerful gifts that come with extending and receiving grace.

Through personal reflection and an engaging activity, you'll have the opportunity to recognize the specific gifts forgiveness has brought into your life. The section concludes with a guided prayer of gratitude, allowing you to thank God for the blessings that forgiveness offers.

THE GIFTS AND BENEFITS OF FORGIVENESS

Forgiveness is not only a commandment but also a powerful gift from God that brings many blessings into our lives. As you embrace forgiveness, you are not only repairing broken connections but also experiencing spiritual growth, answered prayers, and God's mercy and grace.

Let these verses encourage you to recognize the transformative power of forgiveness and the abundant blessings that flow from it.

Peace - Colossians 3:15
"Let the peace of Christ rule in your hearts, to which indeed you were called in one body; and be thankful."

Restored Relationships - Colossians 3:13
"Bearing with one another, and forgiving each other, whoever has a complaint against anyone; just as the Lord forgave you, so also should you."

Spiritual Growth - Ephesians 4:32
"Be kind to one another, tender-hearted, forgiving each other, just as God in Christ also has forgiven you."

Answered Prayers - Mark 11:25
"Whenever you stand praying, forgive, if you have anything against anyone, so that your Father who is in heaven will also forgive you your transgressions."

Mercy and Grace - Matthew 5:7
"Blessed are the merciful, for they shall receive mercy."

Healing - Psalm 147:3
"He heals the brokenhearted and binds up their wounds."

REFLECTING ON THE GIFTS OF FORGIVENESS

Forgiveness and letting go are gifts that offer us much more than just release from pain—they bring peace, freedom, and healing into our lives.

When we forgive, we free ourselves from the weight of bitterness and resentment, allowing inner peace to settle in. It's a quiet, powerful shift, where the burdens of the past no longer have control over us, and we can experience a sense of calm and clarity.

Letting go also opens the door to deep emotional healing. As we forgive, we create space for restoration within ourselves. **The wounds caused by hurtful experiences begin to heal, bringing relief and renewal to our spirits.** It is a profound gift that allows us to move forward with a lighter, more hopeful heart.

Beyond personal healing, forgiveness strengthens relationships, fostering unity and understanding. When we choose to forgive, we are choosing connection over division, grace over judgment. This act not only brings healing to others but deepens our own emotional and spiritual growth, helping us align with love and compassion.

As you go through the next four pages, reflect on the gifts that forgiveness and letting go have brought into your life, and circle any that resonate with your experience.

These gifts—peace, freedom, healing, and more—are the rewards of releasing the past and embracing the freedom that forgiveness offers.

REFLECTING ON THE GIFTS OF FORGIVENESS

As you reflect on your journey of forgiveness and letting go, take a moment to acknowledge the gifts you've received.

Circle or highlight the ones that resonate with your experience.

Increased empathy and compassion for other

Greater emotional resilience

Deepened self-awareness

Enhanced ability to set healthy boundaries

Improved communication skills

Strengthened faith and spiritual connection

Increased capacity for forgiveness

Greater appreciation for life and its challenges

Heightened sense of personal strength and courage

Improved problem-solving skills

Greater ability to navigate difficult emotions

Enhanced creativity and self-expression

Increased self-love and self-acceptance

REFLECTING ON THE GIFTS OF FORGIVENESS

As you reflect on your journey of forgiveness and letting go, take a moment to acknowledge the gifts you've received.

Circle or highlight the ones that resonate with your experience.

Greater ability to trust oneself and one's instincts

Improved relationships with others

Enhanced ability to let go of the past

Greater sense of inner peace and calm

Increased ability to live in the present moment

Enhanced sense of purpose and meaning in life

Greater ability to embrace change and uncertainty

Increased resilience in the face of adversity

Enhanced ability to find joy and gratitude in life

Greater sense of personal freedom and liberation

Improved ability to set and achieve personal goals

Enhanced ability to connect with others on a deeper level

Greater sense of self-sufficiency and independence

REFLECTING ON THE GIFTS OF FORGIVENESS

As you reflect on your journey of forgiveness and letting go, take a moment to acknowledge the gifts you've received.

Circle or highlight the ones that resonate with your experience.

Increased ability to take responsibility for one's own happiness

Enhanced ability to find beauty and inspiration in the world

Greater sense of self-respect and dignity

Improved ability to maintain healthy relationships

Enhanced ability to find meaning and purpose in suffering

Greater sense of inner strength and power

Increased ability to advocate for oneself and others

Enhanced ability to create a positive future

Greater sense of self-awareness and self-knowledge

Improved ability to manage stress and anxiety

Enhanced ability to find hope and optimism in difficult times

Greater sense of personal growth and transformation

Increased ability to inspire and uplift others

REFLECTING ON THE GIFTS OF FORGIVENESS

As you reflect on your journey of forgiveness and letting go, take a moment to acknowledge the gifts you've received.

Circle or highlight the ones that resonate with your experience.

Enhanced ability to create a life of meaning and purpose

Greater sense of self-love and self-care

Improved ability to cultivate inner peace and tranquility

Enhanced ability to find joy and happiness in the present moment

Greater sense of personal freedom and autonomy

Increased ability to create healthy boundaries with others

Enhanced ability to find meaning and purpose in challenges

Greater sense of self-acceptance and self-compassion

Improved ability to let go of anger and resentment

Enhanced ability to find forgiveness and understanding

Greater sense of inner wisdom and guidance

Increased ability to trust in a higher power or divine plan

Enhanced ability to find strength in vulnerability

PRAY

As you reflect on the incredible gifts that forgiveness brings—peace, freedom, healing, and restoration—take a moment to enter into this prayer. Let it be a time to open your heart to God's grace and to fully embrace the blessings that come from offering and receiving forgiveness.

Dear Heavenly Father (Abba),

I come before You, filled with gratitude for the beautiful gifts that forgiveness brings. Thank You for the peace that settles in my heart when I choose to forgive, for the freedom that lifts the weight of resentment from my soul, and for the healing that flows through me as I release the pain I've held onto.

Lord, I thank You for restoring my relationships—both with others and with You—through the grace of forgiveness. I ask that You continue to open my heart to forgive, knowing that in doing so, I grow closer to You. I welcome the spiritual growth that forgiveness brings and trust in Your guidance as I learn to walk this path with humility and love.

Father, let the gifts of forgiveness flow through my life. May Your peace reign in my heart, Your love fill my relationships, and Your grace guide me each step of the way. I trust in Your power to heal, restore, and renew, and I surrender my hurts to You.

In Jesus' name, Amen.

REFLECT

Take a moment to pause and reflect on the powerful gifts that forgiveness brings into your life. As you've prayed and invited God into this journey, consider the peace that begins to fill the spaces once held by bitterness or pain. Forgiveness, both given and received, has the ability to restore your spirit and draw you closer to the heart of God.

What changes are you noticing in your heart as you begin to release past hurts? Perhaps you feel a sense of freedom or lightness, a burden lifted that you didn't even realize you were carrying. This is the freeing power of God's grace at work within you.

Now, consider how these gifts—**peace, freedom, healing, restored relationships**—might continue to unfold in your life. Each time you choose forgiveness, you are choosing to open yourself to God's renewing love. How might this affect your relationships? How could this change the way you see yourself and others?

Remember, forgiveness is not a one-time event, but a process that continues to evolve. God's love and mercy guide you through every step. As you continue to lean into this journey, allow Him to help you let go of anger, resentment, and pain. Trust that He is leading you toward wholeness, toward a life filled with grace and compassion.

Take a moment now to reflect on how you can continue to embrace the gifts of forgiveness. What areas of your life might benefit from this grace? How can you be intentional about choosing peace, healing, and love moving forward?

Let God's presence surround you as you continue this path of forgiveness, trusting that His love will bring you ever closer to the peace and freedom you desire.

SECTION 13

The Power of Apology

In this section, you will explore the power of apologies and their role in a life of forgiveness. Through scripture, you will learn about the significance of seeking forgiveness and offering a sincere, heartfelt apology as a step toward healing and restoration.

You will engage in activities designed to help you practice offering genuine apologies and learn how to find peace when it isn't possible to say the words in person. As you work through this section, you'll discover how apologies can mend broken connections and move you closer to wholeness.

THE POWER OF APOLOGIES IN A LIFE OF FORGIVENESS

Apologies are far more than just words—they are a vital expression of humility, accountability, and a genuine desire to restore what has been broken. Whether we've hurt someone through careless words, failed expectations, or deeper betrayals, offering a sincere apology is one of the first steps toward healing fractured relationships. Apologies are an opportunity for reconciliation and an act of love, but most importantly, they reflect the heart of forgiveness, both human and divine.

In our journey of faith, apologies play a crucial role in living out God's calling for us.

The Bible calls us to love one another, to seek peace, and to live in harmony. Apologizing is an active step toward those goals. It requires us to recognize when we've fallen short and to take responsibility for the hurt we've caused. Just as God graciously forgives us for our sins, we are called to seek forgiveness from those we've wronged and to offer forgiveness to others.

At the heart of every sincere apology is **humility**—the ability to acknowledge that we are not perfect, that we make mistakes, and that we are continually in need of God's grace. When we approach others with a humble heart, willing to admit our faults, we reflect the same grace that God extends to us. The act of apologizing aligns us with the message of the gospel: that through repentance, we find forgiveness and restoration.

But apologies are not just about restoring human relationships—they are also about healing the soul. Carrying the weight of guilt and unspoken apologies can be a burden on our hearts. Seeking forgiveness allows us to free ourselves from that burden, restoring peace within us and drawing us closer to God. **In this way, apologizing is as much about our personal spiritual growth as it is about the relationships we are trying to mend.**

THE POWER OF APOLOGIES IN A LIFE OF FORGIVENESS

Different kinds of apologies play out in our lives—some are simple, like saying "sorry" when we accidentally hurt someone, while others require a deeper level of acknowledgment and healing. Whether you are apologizing for a small slight or a larger transgression, each apology has the power to heal, strengthen, and renew both relationships and our own hearts.

As you reflect on the concept of apologies in your own life, think about the people you've hurt, intentionally or unintentionally, and the apologies that may be long overdue. Consider also the times you've been on the receiving end, and how those moments of reconciliation have helped mend wounds and bring healing.

Apologizing requires courage, but it is through courage that we step into the light of forgiveness—where God meets us with His unending grace.

In the following pages, we will explore the scriptural foundation of forgiveness, practical steps for offering a heartfelt apology, and what to do when saying "I'm sorry" isn't possible.

Each step of this journey will lead you closer to understanding the transformative power of forgiveness and the freedom that comes from releasing guilt and embracing restoration.

SEEKING FORGIVENESS IN SCRIPTURE

Forgiveness is a transformative process, one that requires humility, honesty, and a willingness to change. These verses remind us that forgiveness is not simply a moment, but a heartfelt commitment to understanding, making amends, and growing in grace.

As you read through these passages, reflect on how they can shape the way you seek forgiveness and offer it to others.

Acknowledging the Wrong - Psalm 32:5
"I acknowledged my sin to You, and my iniquity I did not hide; I said, 'I will confess my transgressions to the Lord'; and You forgave the guilt of my sin."

Accepting Responsibility - Psalm 51:4
"Against You, You only, I have sinned and done what is evil in Your sight, so that You are justified when You speak and blameless when You judge."

Expressing Remorse - 2 Corinthians 7:10
"For the sorrow that is according to the will of God produces a repentance without regret, leading to salvation, but the sorrow of the world produces death."

Asking for Forgiveness - 1 John 1:9
"If we confess our sins, He is faithful and righteous to forgive us our sins and to cleanse us from all unrighteousness."

Making Amends - Matthew 5:23-24
"Therefore if you are presenting your offering at the altar, and there remember that your brother has something against you, leave your offering there before the altar and go; first be reconciled to your brother, and then come and present your offering."

THE POWER OF A SINCERE APOLOGY

Expressing genuine remorse and seeking forgiveness are vital steps in restoring relationships and finding inner peace.

Offering a sincere apology requires both humility and a willingness to make amends for the harm caused. A true apology goes beyond words; it reflects a desire to rebuild trust and show that you are committed to change.

Below are key steps to help guide you in offering an apology with sincerity and grace:

Step 1: Own It
The first step is to admit that you have failed or disappointed someone you care about. It's important to avoid deflecting blame by using phrases like, "I'm sorry you feel that way," which shift responsibility onto the other person. Instead, take full responsibility for your actions and acknowledge their impact without excuses.

Step 2: Express Regret
Show genuine sorrow and contrition for your actions or words. A heartfelt apology demonstrates a true change of heart and a commitment to behaving differently in the future. Articulate how you plan to avoid repeating the same mistake—whether that means promising to communicate more effectively or being more considerate of the other person's feelings.

Step 3: Offer Restitution
Consider how you can make amends for your offense. This may involve repairing the damage you caused, offering financial compensation, or performing a meaningful gesture to show your remorse. Taking action shows the other person that you are serious about repairing the relationship.

THE POWER OF A SINCERE APOLOGY

Step 4: Show Understanding
A key part of any apology is showing empathy. Acknowledge the hurt you've caused by saying, "This is how I think I hurt you," and take it a step further by asking, "How else have I hurt you?" This approach shows that you are invested in understanding the full impact of your actions.

Step 5: Ask for Forgiveness
Forgiveness is not something you can demand—it's a gift that the other person offers when they are ready. When asking for forgiveness, express gratitude for their willingness to consider it, and give them the space to process their emotions.

As you consider these steps, take a moment to reflect on who in your life you may owe an apology to.

Is there someone you've hurt, intentionally or unintentionally, who deserves a sincere expression of remorse? It could be a friend, a family member, a coworker, or even yourself. Sometimes, the hardest apology to offer is the one to ourselves—for the times we've believed harmful lies, acted recklessly with our choices or held onto guilt and shame.

Allow yourself to consider where healing is needed and where an apology could be the first step toward restoration, whether with others or within yourself.

AN EXAMPLE OF A SINCERE SELF-APOLOGY

Before crafting your own apology, it can be helpful to see an example that illustrates how to navigate this process.

I acknowledge that I've let myself down by neglecting my well-being and not prioritizing my needs. I take full responsibility for my choices and understand how they have impacted my mental and emotional health. In doing so, I recognize that I have also strayed from the path that God desires for me—a path of love, compassion, and self-care.

I genuinely regret not being kinder to myself and recognize the pain this has caused. It's clear that my actions have led to feelings of unworthiness and sadness, which distance me from the truth of God's love for me. Moving forward, I commit to embracing self-compassion and understanding as I strive to treat myself with the care I deserve, reflecting the love God has for me.

To make amends, I will establish a self-care routine that prioritizes my mental and emotional health, recognizing this as part of my responsibility as God's creation. I will dedicate time each week to engage in activities that nurture my spirit and allow me to reconnect with who I truly am in His eyes.

I understand the weight of my neglect and the impact it has had on my life. I'm aware that by not taking care of myself, I've hindered my true potential from shining through, which is a gift God intended for me to share with the world.

So, I ask for my own forgiveness for the way I've treated myself and for not fully embracing the love God offers me and as he calls me in the Second Commandment to love myself and others. I appreciate this opportunity to reflect, and I promise to embrace the journey of healing and self-acceptance with God's guidance as I move forward.

RESTORING THROUGH APOLOGY

Now that you've reflected on who may be in need of your apology—whether it's another person or yourself—take a moment to apply the steps you just learned. Craft a sincere apology by owning your actions, expressing genuine regret, and showing understanding for the impact of your behavior. Consider how you can make amends and ask for forgiveness with humility and grace.

Whether this apology is one you plan to deliver to someone else or a way to offer forgiveness to yourself, take the time to write it thoughtfully and from the heart.

Step 1: Own It

Step 2: Express Regret

RESTORING THROUGH APOLOGY

Step 3: Offer Restitution

Step 4: Show Understanding

Step 5: Ask for Forgiveness

WHEN IT ISN'T POSSIBLE TO SAY THE WORDS

There are times when expressing remorse and seeking forgiveness directly from the person you've hurt is impossible, unhealthy, or unwise. Even in these situations, you can still find healing and release through spiritual practices. These exercises can help you process your emotions, find peace, and entrust the relationship to God.

Prayerful Confession
In a quiet space, acknowledge your wrongdoing before God. Be specific about your actions and their impact, expressing sincere remorse. Ask for God's forgiveness and guidance in making things right. This is an essential step in seeking inner healing, even when direct communication isn't possible.

Journaling
Write a letter to the person you've hurt, apologizing and sharing the insights you've gained. Be honest about your feelings and your commitment to change. Even if you never send the letter, this exercise can help you process emotions and find closure.

Visualization
In a state of prayerful meditation, imagine having a conversation with the person you've wronged. Express your apology, and visualize them responding with understanding and forgiveness. This practice can help you find inner peace and release lingering guilt or shame.

Making Amends Indirectly
If direct restitution is not possible, find ways to make amends indirectly. This might include volunteering, donating to a relevant charity, or supporting a cause that aligns with the values you compromised. By taking positive action, you demonstrate your commitment to growth and healing.

WHEN IT ISN'T POSSIBLE TO SAY THE WORDS

Forgiveness Meditation
In a quiet, reflective space, focus on God's unconditional love and forgiveness. Imagine this love surrounding you and filling your heart. Extend this same compassion and forgiveness to yourself, acknowledging that you are a work in progress. Release any self-judgment and embrace the peace that comes with self-forgiveness.

Surrendering the Relationship
In prayer, consciously surrender the broken relationship to God. Recognize that you cannot control the other person's response or the outcome. Trust that God will work for the good of all involved, and release the burden of trying to fix things on your own.

> Remember, healing and forgiveness are a journey, not a destination.

By engaging in these spiritual practices and entrusting your broken relationships to God, you invite the transformative power of divine love and grace into your life. As you continue to seek growth and alignment with God's will, trust that He will guide you toward peace and reconciliation—both within yourself and in your relationships with others.

PRAY

This guided prayer invites you to reflect on the power of humility, seek God's guidance in offering sincere apologies, and embrace His healing grace.

Dear Heavenly Father (Abba),

I come before You with a heart that longs for healing, restoration, and peace. I thank You for Your endless grace and forgiveness, and I ask for the courage to reflect that same grace to others in my life. Help me to approach my relationships with humility, recognizing when I have caused pain or hurt, and guide me as I seek reconciliation.

Lord, I know that apologizing requires strength and honesty. Give me the wisdom to own my mistakes fully and the humility to ask for forgiveness where I have fallen short. Help me to recognize the impact of my words and actions, and give me the grace to apologize sincerely and with a heart that longs for true restoration.

I lift up to You the names of those I have hurt, intentionally or unintentionally. You know the places where reconciliation is needed. I ask that You go before me, softening hearts and preparing the way for healing. Where it is not possible to speak the words of apology in person, help me to find peace in offering these apologies to You, knowing that You see my heart and intentions.

Father, I also pray for the strength to forgive myself. Remind me that I am not defined by my mistakes, but by Your love and mercy. Help me to release the weight of guilt and shame, and to embrace the freedom that comes with Your forgiveness.

May my life be a reflection of Your love, a testament to the power of humility, grace, and reconciliation.

In Jesus' name, Amen.

REFLECT

Take a moment to reflect on the journey of forgiveness.

Apologizing and seeking forgiveness can feel difficult and vulnerable, but remember—you are never walking this path alone. God is with you every step of the way, offering His grace to guide, heal, and strengthen you.

Consider how humility plays a vital role in this process. A true apology is not only an acknowledgment of wrongs but also a humble gift extended to others and yourself. As you reflect on the times God has forgiven you, think about how He continually reaches out to restore your heart, welcoming you back with open arms. His forgiveness is a gift freely given, and it is through His love that you are empowered to extend forgiveness to others, even when it feels challenging or undeserved.

Reflect on how this transformative process is shaping your character. How has receiving God's forgiveness helped you to view yourself with more compassion and understanding? In what ways might inviting Him deeper into your journey equip you with the strength needed to make amends and foster healing in your relationships?

Remember, forgiveness transcends mere words; it embodies a heart posture willing to release anger and resentment. It involves offering grace, even when it's difficult. God's grace empowers you to forgive, to be forgiven, and to grow through this journey.

Let His love continue to work in your heart as you move forward, trusting that with Him, healing is always possible.

SECTION 14

Steps Toward Reconciliation

In this section, explore the path of rebuilding relationships through reconciliation. We look at the vital importance of restoring trust, mutual understanding, and genuine connection after forgiveness.

Reconciliation takes the healing process a step further by focusing on the careful rebuilding of relationships, guided by biblical principles and practical wisdom. With a foundation of grace, empathy, and respect, this journey will offer insights into how to foster deeper connections that honor God and strengthen bonds.

REBUILDING THROUGH RECONCILIATION

Reconciliation plays a powerful role in the journey of forgiveness, inviting us to not only release the past but also restore relationships in a way that honors both ourselves and others.

While forgiveness is an inner process of releasing resentment, reconciliation goes a step further, rebuilding trust, mutual understanding, and connection. This part of the journey reflects the heart of God's design for relationships, allowing us to foster deeper, more honest bonds where healing and respect can flourish.

Reconciliation requires patience, humility, and intentional effort from both parties involved. It's a process that seeks to address past hurts with honesty and openness, creating a path toward renewed understanding and connection.

As Proverbs 4:23 reminds us, *"Watch over your heart with all diligence, for from it flow the springs of life."* This wisdom encourages us to engage in reconciliation carefully and mindfully, using boundaries to protect our emotional well-being. In doing so, we create space for healing while honoring our needs and values.

The Role of Boundaries in Reconciliation

Boundaries are essential to the reconciliation process. They act as guides that help protect us from repeated harm, while also setting the framework for respectful interactions. Boundaries enable us to forgive without compromising our emotional safety, allowing us to honor ourselves as we offer grace to others.

Importantly, boundaries are not static; they can adapt as trust grows or shift as situations change, but they continue to serve as a foundation for maintaining mutual respect and safety in our relationships.

REBUILDING THROUGH RECONCILIATION

Forgiveness does not mean forgetting the past or allowing harmful behaviors to persist. Instead, boundaries help us communicate clearly, reinforcing what we need to feel safe and valued. In this way, boundaries become a tool for authentic connection, ensuring that both people involved understand each other's limits and responsibilities. By maintaining these guidelines, we allow reconciliation to unfold in a way that is compassionate and safe.

Building on Trust, Empathy, and Communication

Healthy communication, trust, and empathy are central to meaningful reconciliation. Communication allows us to express needs openly and practice active listening—showing presence without judgment. This helps both people feel seen and valued.

Trust, essential for reconciliation, is rebuilt gradually through consistent, respectful actions. Each step toward honesty strengthens the relationship and deepens understanding. Empathy, too, allows us to extend compassion, seeing the other person's perspective and reflecting Christ's love, even amid difficulty.

Seeking Support in the Journey

Reconciliation is often complex, and seeking guidance from a counselor, faith leader, or trusted advisor can be helpful. Support can offer tools for communication, boundary-setting, and managing challenging emotions, keeping the reconciliation process respectful and grounded in growth.

While relationships may not return to their original state, reconciliation provides a path for new, healthier connections. Embrace this journey as an opportunity for healing, peace, and grace-filled transformation.

PRAY

Take a moment to quiet your heart and invite God into this space. This guided prayer is an opportunity to ask for His guidance as you seek reconciliation, healing, and restored connections in your life. Open your heart to Him, and let His presence lead you through this process.

Dear Heavenly Father (Abba),

I come to You with a heart that longs for healing and restoration. You know the places in my life where trust has been broken and relationships have suffered. Lord, I want to rebuild these connections, but I need Your help. Teach me how to reconcile in a way that honors You—how to rebuild trust, seek understanding, and move forward with love and respect.

Help me to listen with an open heart, not just to respond, but to truly understand the feelings and perspectives of those I need to reconcile with. Guide my words, that they may reflect grace and patience, and lead me to speak with kindness even when it's difficult.

Lord, I ask for wisdom in setting boundaries that protect my heart and the hearts of others. Help me respect those boundaries, knowing they are part of healthy, Godly relationships. As I move forward, remind me that reconciliation is a process, one that requires time, patience, and most of all, Your presence.

I trust You to guide this journey, knowing that You are a God of connection and restoration. Help me to move forward in a way that reflects Your love—building relationships that honor You and bring peace to my life and to others.

In Jesus' name, Amen.

REFLECT

Take a moment to reflect on the path of reconciliation.

Rebuilding relationships, whether through listening, setting boundaries, or working toward mutual understanding, is not always easy. But remember—God is the source of your strength and peace, walking with you through each step of this journey. His desire for reconciliation mirrors the ways He continually seeks to restore your relationship with Him.

Consider how God is calling you to approach others with the same grace and love He has shown you. As you work through listening with empathy, respecting boundaries, and fostering healthier communication, think about the ways God has already demonstrated these principles in your life. He listens to your heart without judgment, respects your needs, and patiently guides you toward healing.

Reconciliation is a process that takes time, patience, and openness. It involves not only speaking but also hearing the other person's heart, and creating a space where both parties can feel safe and valued. How has God invited you to show this kind of compassion in your relationships? How might these efforts to rebuild trust reflect the deeper reconciliation God seeks with each of us?

Allow this time of reflection to shape your heart as you move forward. Remember that with God's help, reconciliation can lead to deeper, more meaningful connections, grounded in the love and grace He extends to us all.

Take comfort in knowing that as you seek to rebuild with others, you are growing into the person God has called you to be—**one who reflects His love, peace, and forgiveness.**

SECTION 15

Learning to Live Blamelessly

This section explores the meaning of living blamelessly in alignment with God's teachings. Through reflection and introspection, you'll begin to understand how striving for a blameless life can lead to spiritual growth, healing, and a deeper connection with God.

You will engage in a self-reflection activity, followed by the creation of a personal action plan that encourages living in harmony with God's will. A concluding prayer will guide you toward maintaining this mindset in your daily life.

LEARNING TO LIVE BLAMELESSLY

While forgiveness is a cornerstone of the Christian faith, the Bible also teaches us to live in a way that minimizes the need for forgiveness. This involves being intentional in our actions, considering their impact on others, and striving to live blamelessly as a reflection of Christ's transformative power.

What Does It Mean to Live Blamelessly?

Living blamelessly doesn't mean living perfectly, but it means striving to live in a way that reflects Christ's love and avoids causing unnecessary harm to others. It's about being mindful of how your actions, words, and decisions affect those around you and intentionally living as a witness to the transformative power of the gospel. Let's explore how this is done.

Self-Awareness
Regularly examine your actions and consider how they may affect others. Ask yourself: Am I acting with kindness, patience, and love? A blameless life starts with recognizing where we may unintentionally cause harm and choosing to align ourselves with Christ's example.

Responsibility
Freedom in Christ comes with responsibility. Living blamelessly means balancing personal freedoms with care for the spiritual growth of others. Consider how your actions could influence those around you, especially those who may be newer or more vulnerable in their faith.

Wisdom
A blameless life requires wisdom—discerning how best to navigate potential areas of conflict or misunderstanding. Seek God's guidance in your decisions, especially when your choices might impact others. This wisdom helps you act thoughtfully and avoid unnecessary harm.

LEARNING TO LIVE BLAMELESSLY

Love

At the core of living blamelessly is love. When you prioritize love, you naturally act in ways that foster unity and protect the well-being of others. Christ's love compels us to treat others with grace, compassion, and humility. Ask yourself: Am I acting in love for my neighbor and for the good of the community?

Witness

Your life is a testament to your faith. Living blamelessly is about demonstrating Christ's influence on your life in everything you do. When others see your integrity, kindness, and care for others, you become a reflection of Christ's love and a light in the world.

The Journey Toward Blameless Living

While we acknowledge our imperfections and our ongoing need for God's grace, striving to live blamelessly is a worthy pursuit for every believer.

By being mindful of our actions and their impact, we can minimize the need for forgiveness and more effectively reflect Christ's love to the world.

Remember, this journey is ongoing. It requires vigilance, prayer, and a reliance on the guidance of the Holy Spirit. As we grow in this area, we reduce the need for forgiveness, strengthen our witness, and promote unity within the body of Christ.

A SELF-REFLECTION AND ACTION PLAN

Living blamelessly requires a deeper awareness of how your actions affect others and a commitment to making thoughtful, Christ-centered decisions.

This activity will guide you through reflecting on a single significant action and developing practical strategies, grounded in biblical principles, to minimize the need for forgiveness. By fostering greater self-awareness and intentionality, you can build healthier relationships and reflect Christ's love more fully in every aspect of your life.

Step 1: Self-Reflection on a Signification Action

Choose one significant decision or action you've taken recently. Reflect deeply on this action and answer the following questions:

- How did this action affect others around me?
- Could this action have caused someone to stumble in their faith or been negatively impacted? If so, how?
- What alternative action could I have taken to avoid any negative impact?

A SELF-REFLECTION AND ACTION PLAN

Step 2: Impact Assessment and Action Plan

Identify one key area of your life where this action might have a ripple effect (e.g., family, work, church, social media). For this area:

- What potential stumbling blocks or offenses could this action create
- Develop 2-3 specific strategies you could use to minimize similar risks in the future.
- Choose a Bible verse that can serve as a guide for your behavior in this situation.

A SELF-REFLECTION AND ACTION PLAN

Step 3: Personal Growth and Reflection

Reflect on what you've learned from this process. Are there patterns or habits that this action revealed, and how can you be more mindful in the future?

_____
_____
_____
_____
_____
_____
_____
_____
_____
_____
_____
_____
_____
_____

Step 4: Holding Yourself Accountable

Commit to a weekly self-check-in, reviewing your progress and adjusting your strategies as needed to ensure growth in living blamelessly. Aim to continue this practice for at least one month, using the check-in sheet to hold yourself accountable.

WEEKLY CHECK IN SHEET

Week 1:

Week 2:

Week 3:

Week 4:

Additional Notes:

PRAY

As you read this prayer, invite God to guide you toward living a life that reflects His love and grace in all you do.

Dear Heavenly Father (Abba),

I come before You with a heart that longs to live in a way that reflects Your goodness and grace. Thank You for the gift of Your guidance, Your endless love, and the wisdom You continue to pour into my life. Help me to walk the path of righteousness, always mindful of how my actions and words affect those around me. I know that, on my own, I fall short—but through Your strength, I can learn to walk blamelessly, guided by Your Spirit.

Lord, teach me to be more aware of the impact I have on others. Show me where I have caused harm, knowingly or unknowingly, and give me the humility to seek forgiveness. May I be quick to listen, slow to speak, and slow to anger, reflecting Your heart in all I do. When I stumble, remind me that Your grace is always there to lift me back up.

Father, I ask for the strength to make choices that honor You and bring peace into my relationships. Help me to discern when to act, when to speak, and when to remain still, trusting in Your timing and Your will. Shape me into a person who brings healing and restoration, and give me the courage to stand up for what is right with a spirit of love and grace.

As I continue this journey, grant me the patience to embrace change, the wisdom to grow, and the courage to let go of anything that does not reflect Your will. Help me to forgive myself for my mistakes and to extend that same forgiveness to others. Let my life be a testament to Your transforming power, that in all things, I would bring glory to Your name.

Keep my heart pure, my hands clean, and my intentions aligned with Your purpose. Walk with me daily, Lord, as I seek to live a life that is blameless in Your sight, not by my own efforts, but through the work of Your Spirit within me.

In Jesus' name, Amen.

REFLECT

Living blamelessly is not about perfection but about pursuing a heart aligned with God's will. It's about daily choices that reflect integrity, humility, and compassion.

Take this time to reflect on your journey so far. What steps have you already taken toward living a life that honors God? Where do you still feel the pull of old habits or actions that don't align with the blameless life He calls you to?

Ask yourself how embracing this call to live blamelessly might change your interactions with others.

Are there areas of your life where you've been hesitant to let God lead? And, just as important, how can you lean on His strength when the pursuit of living blamelessly feels overwhelming?

Living this way doesn't happen overnight.

Each day, as you bring these areas to God, know that your obedience and discipline are acts of faith that draw you closer to Him. Consistency in seeking His guidance and submitting to His will is the path to transformation.

As you continue on this journey, remember that these small, faithful steps are renewing your mind and shaping your heart to reflect His love. Even when progress seems slow, trust that God is working within you, creating lasting change that leads to freedom.

Keep coming back to Him, seeking guidance and grace. His desire is not for perfection but for your faithful pursuit of His ways, step by step.

SECTION 16

Caring for Body and Soul

This section emphasizes the crucial role of self-care in the forgiveness journey. You'll explore how nurturing your physical, emotional, and spiritual well-being supports the healing process and helps release negativity. Caring for yourself is not only essential for healing but also for maintaining the ongoing practice of forgiveness in your life.

Engage in practical self-care activities, including spiritual renewal exercises, physical stretches for emotional release, and journaling. You'll also learn about nutrition, biblical wisdom and knowledge, and modern healing to support holistic well-being, ensuring that you are equipped to continually practice forgiveness and live in peace.

THE ROLE OF SELF-CARE IN FORGIVENESS

In 1 Corinthians 6:19, we are reminded that our bodies are temples of the Holy Spirit. *"Or do you not know that your body is a temple of the Holy Spirit who is in you, whom you have from God, and that you are not your own?"* **This truth calls us to honor God not only in spirit but also through how we care for ourselves physically.**

This concept ties closely to the second greatest commandment given by Jesus in Matthew 22:39: *'You shall love your neighbor as yourself.'* While this commandment emphasizes loving others, it inherently calls us to love and care for ourselves as well. If we are to love our neighbors well, we must first practice love and care toward ourselves. Self-care, then, becomes an extension of this commandment, enabling us to reflect God's love outward by first tending to our own well-being.

When we hold onto unforgiveness, our bodies often bear the burden.

Physical tension, stress, and emotional weight can manifest in ways that drain us, leaving us unable to show up fully for others or ourselves. By incorporating self-care practices into our forgiveness journey—whether through physical movement, rest, or mindfulness—we honor the temple that God has entrusted to us.

Caring for our bodies is an act of love that allows us to release burdens, restore balance, and make space for God's peace. **This self-care is not selfish; it is essential.** Through it, we cultivate strength to continue the work of forgiveness and to reflect the love of God in all we do—both for ourselves and for others.

As you engage with the practices in this section, remember that in caring for your body, you are also honoring God, aligning with His commandment to love yourself as He loves you.

SCRIPTURES FOR REST, RENEWAL AND PEACE

During times of forgiveness and grief, self-care becomes essential as we navigate the emotional and spiritual challenges of healing. The following scriptures remind us that our bodies are temples of the Holy Spirit and that we are called to honor God through rest, renewal, and peace, even in difficult seasons. These verses encourage us to embrace self-care by seeking quiet moments with God, allowing Him to refresh our souls and bring peace to our hearts.

1 Corinthians 6:19-20
"Do you not know that your bodies are temples of the Holy Spirit, who is in you, whom you have received from God? You are not your own; you were bought at a price. Therefore honor God with your bodies."

Mark 6:31
"Then, because so many people were coming and going that they did not even have a chance to eat, he said to them, 'Come with me by yourselves to a quiet place and get some rest.'"

Proverbs 17:22
"A cheerful heart is good medicine, but a crushed spirit dries up the bones."

Philippians 4:6-7
"Do not be anxious about anything, but in every situation, by prayer and petition, with thanksgiving, present your requests to God. And the peace of God, which transcends all understanding, will guard your hearts and your minds in Christ Jesus."

Psalm 23:1-3
"The Lord is my shepherd, I lack nothing. He makes me lie down in green pastures, he leads me beside quiet waters, he refreshes my soul."

ACTIVITIES FOR SPIRITUAL RENEWAL

As we embrace the importance of self-care in our healing journey, it's essential to remember that nurturing our souls involves more than just physical rest.

It's about creating intentional moments to connect with God, care for our hearts, and find peace in His presence. These activities are designed to provide spaces of renewal, where your spirit can be refreshed, your mind can find calm, and your body can feel cared for. Each activity is paired with a song that can serve as a backdrop to help you center your thoughts on God and His goodness.

Feel free to adapt these practices to your own needs—whether it's a quiet moment of meditation or a time of creative expression, each is meant to draw you closer to God's love and peace.

Guided Scripture Meditation

Choose a comforting Bible passage (e.g., Psalm 23 or Philippians 4:6-7). Find a quiet place, close your eyes, and slowly read or listen to the verses. Reflect on each word, allowing its meaning to sink in. Visualize the scene or emotions described. Spend 15-20 minutes in this peaceful reflection.

Song: *"You Say"* by Lauren Daigle

Nature Prayer Walk

Take a slow walk in a park or natural setting. As you walk, pray about your feelings and challenges. Notice the beauty around you—leaves, flowers, sky—and thank God for these creations. Use nature as a metaphor for your journey of healing and growth.

Song: *"So Will I (100 Billion X)"* by Hillsong United

ACTIVITIES FOR SPIRITUAL RENEWAL

Gratitude Jar

Get a large jar and some colorful paper. Each day, write down one thing you're grateful for, no matter how small. During tough times, read through these notes to remind yourself of life's blessings.

Song: *"Goodness of God"* by Jenn Johnson

Gentle Stretching or Somatic Movement

Combine gentle stretches with Christian meditation. As you move, focus on Bible verses or pray. This practice connects body, mind, and spirit, bringing relaxation and reflection.

Song: *"It Is Well"* by Bethel Music & Kristene DiMarco

Art and Worship

Create a piece of art (painting, collage, drawing) while listening to worship music. Let the music inspire your creation. Don't focus on perfection—let it be an expression of your emotions and faith.

Song: *"Reckless Love"* by Cory Asbury

Comfort Food Cooking

Prepare a nourishing meal that reminds you of God's provision. As you cook, pray over the ingredients. Invite a friend to share the meal, or enjoy it mindfully on your own, savoring each bite as a gift from God.

Song: *"The Table"* by Chris Tomlin

ACTIVITIES FOR SPIRITUAL RENEWAL

Letter to God

Write an honest, heartfelt letter to God expressing all your feelings—anger, sadness, hope, gratitude. Pour out your heart without censoring yourself.

Song: *"Dear God"* by Cory Asbury

Memory Stone Ritual

Collect a smooth stone. Write a word representing something you're releasing on one side, and a word representing a truth you're embracing on the other. Hold it during prayer times, and eventually place it in a special spot as a reminder of your journey.

Song: *"Another in the Fire"* by Hillsong United

Spiritual Vision Board

Create a collage of images and words that represent your hopes, dreams, and the person you're becoming through this process. Include Bible verses that speak to you. Place it where you'll see it daily.

Song: *"The Blessing"* by Kari Jobe, Cody Carnes, and Elevation Worship

ACTIVITIES FOR SPIRITUAL RENEWAL

Anointing Oil Meditation

Get some anointing oil (or olive oil that has been set aside and consecrated). In a quiet moment, place a drop on your forehead or hands. As you do, pray for healing, forgiveness, or strength. Let the scent and sensation remind you of God's presence throughout your day.

Song: *"Holy Spirit"* by Francesca Battistelli

Remember, self-care is a personal journey.

Feel free to adjust these activities to meet your needs, and let the music inspire your connection to God. Each moment of care, reflection, and prayer is a step toward deeper peace and renewal in His presence.

Move with Purpose.

Heal with Grace.

"MOVING" TOWARDS FORGIVENESS

"For you created my inmost being; you knit me together in my mother's womb." (Psalm 139:13)

In the sacred tapestry of our lives, the intertwining of body, mind, and spirit is an essential truth that we often overlook. As you embark on the transformative journey of forgiveness, it's vital to recognize how your physical well-being directly influences your emotional state. Forgiveness is not merely a mental exercise; it is a profound emotional process that reverberates through every fiber of our being.

The **mind-body connection** plays a pivotal role in this journey. When we hold onto grudges or unresolved anger, we create tension that can manifest physically as stress, fatigue, and discomfort. Just as Scripture teaches us to honor our bodies as temples (1 Corinthians 6:19-20), we must also nurture them through movement and care. The Apostle Paul reminds us that our bodies are not just vessels; **they are sacred spaces, created to glorify God**. In understanding that our bodies house the Holy Spirit, we realize the importance of treating them with respect and care, especially when navigating challenging emotions like forgiveness.

In this section, you will discover how gentle stretching exercises, purposeful breathing practices, and the intimate ritual of washing feet can unlock the path to emotional release. These practices are not just routines; **they are sacred acts that invite healing, humility, and connection**. By integrating movement into your self-care regimen, you allow yourself to let go of the burdens you carry, creating space for grace and healing.

As you engage in these activities, remember that they reflect the very essence of forgiveness—transformative, redemptive, and deeply rooted in love. **Allow your body to move, release, and heal, and watch how this journey of physical self-care enriches your heart and spirit.**

GENTLE EXERCISES FOR EMOTIONAL RELEASE

Simple stretches offer an effective way to release tension stored in the body, making space for emotional healing and forgiveness. As you work through these exercises, remember that this is not only about physical relief but also about creating room for peace in your heart and mind.

Here are a few tips to keep in mind as you begin:

- Breathe deeply and slowly throughout the stretch to enhance relaxation.
- Avoid jerking or sudden movements to prevent injury and protect your body.
- Incorporate these stretches into your daily routine to continually reduce tension and support your forgiveness journey.

Remember to listen to your body during each stretch, and never force yourself into any position that feels uncomfortable. The goal is to release tension and encourage relaxation, not to push beyond your limits.

Shoulder Stretch

This stretch targets the shoulder muscles, promoting relaxation and improving flexibility in the shoulders and upper back.

- Stand or sit with your back straight and shoulders relaxed.
- Reach your right arm across your chest.
- Use your left hand to gently pull your right arm closer to your body.
- Hold the stretch for 15-30 seconds, breathing deeply.
- Slowly release the stretch.
- Repeat on the left side, reaching your left arm across your chest.
- Use your right hand to gently pull your left arm closer.
- Hold for 15-30 seconds, then release.
- Perform 2-3 sets on each side.

GENTLE EXERCISES FOR EMOTIONAL RELEASE

<u>Neck Stretch</u>

This stretch helps release tension in the neck and shoulders, which are common areas for holding stress.

- Sit or stand with your back straight and shoulders relaxed.
- Tilt your head to the right, bringing your right ear toward your right shoulder.
- To deepen the stretch, gently place your right hand on the left side of your head and apply light pressure.
- Hold for 15-30 seconds, breathing deeply.
- Slowly return your head to the center.
- Repeat on the left side, tilting your head to the left.
- Next, gently lower your chin to your chest to stretch the back of your neck.
- Hold for 15-30 seconds, then slowly lift your head back to the center.
- Repeat the entire sequence 2-3 times.

<u>Chest Opener</u>

This stretch helps release tightness in the chest and improve posture, counteracting the forward slouch that can develop from sitting or using devices.

- Stand with your feet shoulder-width apart.
- Clasp your hands behind your back and straighten your arms.
- Lift your clasped hands upward and away from your back.
- Push your chest forward and up while gently tilting your chin up.
- Hold this position for 15-30 seconds, breathing deeply throughout.
- Slowly release the stretch, lowering your arms.
- Repeat 2-3 times.

GENTLE EXERCISES FOR EMOTIONAL RELEASE

Forward Bend

This stretch alleviates tension in the lower back and hamstrings, while lengthening the spine, hamstrings, and calves.

- Stand with your feet hip-width apart.
- Inhale deeply, raising your arms overhead.
- As you exhale, slowly bend forward from your hips, keeping your back straight.
- Let your arms and head hang down toward the floor.
- Bend your knees slightly if you feel tension in your hamstrings.
- Try to bring your fingertips or palms to the floor. If you can't reach, grab your ankles or calves.
- Hold the position for 30-60 seconds, breathing deeply.
- To come up, slowly roll up vertebra by vertebra, with your head coming up last.
- Repeat 2-3 times.

Incorporating simple stretches into your routine can significantly enhance your journey toward emotional healing and forgiveness. Each stretch serves not only as a means to release physical tension but also as a gentle reminder to cultivate peace within yourself. **As you engage in these practices, take a moment to reflect on how releasing tightness in your body can mirror the emotional burdens you carry.**

Embrace the connection between your physical well-being and your emotional state, allowing each stretch to be an opportunity for renewal. Remember, the path to forgiveness is as much about nurturing your body as it is about tending to your spirit.

Embrace this time for yourself, and honor your progress, no matter how small.

BREATH AS DIVINE CONNECTION

The name **YHWH**, often pronounced **"Yahweh,"** is the personal name of God in the Hebrew Bible. This name, known as the Tetragrammaton, is considered so sacred in Jewish tradition that it is often not pronounced aloud. Some scholars and spiritual thinkers have suggested that the pronunciation of YHWH may resemble the sound of breathing itself. This idea invites a deep, spiritual connection between the act of breathing and the presence of God.

When Moses asked for God's name in Exodus 3:14, God replied, *"I AM WHO I AM,"* a declaration closely related to YHWH. This response highlights God's eternal presence and existence—concepts that are intimately tied to the rhythm of breath. With each inhalation and exhalation, we are reminded of God's constant presence in our lives.

The Greek word **"pneuma"** (transliterated as **"nooma"**) carries multiple related meanings: breath, spirit, and wind. This concept appears throughout the New Testament, often referring to the Holy Spirit or the spiritual essence of life.

Genesis 2:7 tells us, *"Then the Lord God formed man of dust from the ground, and breathed into his nostrils the breath of life; and man became a living being."* In this moment, the breath of God is the source of life itself, illustrating the divine power contained in each breath we take.

The apostle Paul emphasizes this in Acts 17:25, stating that God *"gives to all people life and breath and all things."* This reminds us that every breath is a gift from God, connecting us to His life-giving presence.

With these biblical connections in mind, we can begin to see breathing as more than just a biological function—it is a spiritual practice. **Each breath becomes an opportunity to connect with God, receiving His life-giving spirit with each inhale and participating in His ongoing creative power with each exhale.**

BREATHING AS A SPIRITUAL PRACTICE

The following exercises are designed to help you cultivate this connection between breath, spirit, and the divine. As you engage in these practices, approach them with reverence and an open heart, inviting God's presence to fill each moment.

Exercise 1: Contemplative Breath Awareness

- Sit comfortably and close your eyes.
- Breathe naturally and focus on the sound and sensation of your breath.
- As you inhale, silently think "Yah" or imagine the sound of inhaling as "Yah."
- As you exhale, think "Weh" or imagine the sound of exhaling as "Weh."
- Continue for 5-10 minutes, letting each breath remind you of your connection to God.

Exercise 2: Pneuma Breathing

- Sit or lie down comfortably.
- Inhale deeply through your nose for 4 counts.
- Hold the breath for 4 counts.
- Exhale slowly through your mouth for 6 counts, envisioning the release of "pneuma" or divine breath.
- Repeat this cycle for 5-10 minutes, focusing on the sacredness of each breath.

These simple yet powerful exercises invite you to experience the divine presence through the act of breathing. With each breath, you draw closer to God's spirit, receiving His peace and life-giving power.

A RITUAL OF HUMILITY AND FORGIVENESS

In the teachings of Jesus, the act of foot washing stands as a profound symbol of humility, love, and service.

In John 13:14-15, Jesus instructs His disciples: *"If I then, the Lord and the Teacher, washed your feet, you also ought to wash one another's feet. For I gave you an example that you also should do as I did to you."*

This powerful message encourages us to embody the spirit of forgiveness by serving others and ourselves with compassion and grace.

The Foot-Washing Ritual invites you to engage in a meaningful practice that honors and repeats what Jesus modeled for us. Whether you choose to wash your own feet or those of a loved one, this ritual serves as a reminder of our shared humanity and the importance of humility in our forgiveness journey.

Materials Needed

- A basin or bowl of warm water
- A towel
- Optional: Foot soak or essential oils for added relaxation

Step 1: Create a Sacred Space

Find a quiet place where you can engage in this ritual without distractions. You may want to light a candle or play soft music to create a peaceful atmosphere. Consider using 528 Hz healing music, known as the "Love Frequency," to enhance the atmosphere and promote feelings of love, peace, and healing, setting the tone for the ritual.

A RITUAL OF HUMILITY AND FORGIVENESS

Step 2: Prepare Yourself

Take a moment to center yourself through prayer or deep breathing. Ask God to prepare your heart for this act of humility and service, and to reveal any areas of unforgiveness you may need to address.

Step 3: Set Up the Ritual

Fill the basin with warm water. If desired, add a few drops of essential oils for a soothing scent. Consider using oils commonly associated with anointing and spiritual practices, such as:

- Frankincense: Known for its grounding and calming properties, it helps create a sense of peace and connection to the divine.
- Myrrh: Often used for its healing properties and rich historical significance, myrrh promotes emotional balance and tranquility.
- Cypress: Associated with purification, cypress oil can enhance feelings of stability and renewal.
- Lavender: Renowned for its calming effects, lavender encourages relaxation and a sense of peace.
- Rosemary: Known for its uplifting and clarifying properties, rosemary can help with mental clarity and focus during the ritual.

Place the towel nearby for drying.

Step 4: Engage in Reflection

Before you begin washing feet, take a few moments to reflect on the significance of this act. Consider how Jesus modeled servant leadership and how washing someone's feet can represent letting go of pride and judgment.

A RITUAL OF HUMILITY AND FORGIVENESS

Step 5: Wash Your Feet (or a Loved One's)

If washing your own feet, gently place them in the warm water and take your time to soak and cleanse them. As you wash, visualize releasing any burdens or resentment that may be weighing you down.

If washing a loved one's feet, invite them to sit comfortably. Gently wash their feet, focusing on the act of serving and loving them. Use this time to express any feelings of forgiveness or gratitude that may arise.

Step 6: Dry and Bless

After washing, dry the feet with the towel, treating this act with reverence. Whether you are washing your own feet or those of a loved one, take a moment to offer a blessing or words of affirmation, emphasizing the significance of humility and love. Here's a template you can adapt:

Blessing Template: "As I wash your feet, [Name], I honor you in the same way Jesus honored His disciples. May this act of service remind us both of our inherent worth and the love that surrounds us. Just as Jesus demonstrated humility, may we both walk in the spirit of forgiveness and grace, releasing any burdens that hold us back from experiencing God's love.

If washing your own feet, say to yourself: 'As I care for my own feet, I embrace the same humility and love that Jesus showed. I recognize my value and commit to extending kindness to myself, letting go of past grievances and stepping forward in peace.'

May we both step forward with renewed strength, embodying the love of Christ in all we do."

A RITUAL OF HUMILITY AND FORGIVENESS

Step 7: Closing Prayer

Conclude the ritual with a prayer that reinforces the core values of the foot-washing ritual—humility, forgiveness, and service.

"Heavenly Father, thank You for this moment of reflection and service. In washing feet—I am reminded of Jesus' example of humility and the call to serve one another with love. Guide my feet today to be swift in pursuing peace and slow in running toward conflict.

Help us both to carry this spirit of forgiveness into our lives, letting go of pride and embracing the shared humanity we all possess. May Your grace fill our hearts, guiding us to extend kindness and understanding to ourselves and to each other.

As we move forward, let this act of love inspire our journey toward healing and wholeness, reflecting Your love in all that we do. In Jesus' name, Amen."

Engaging in the Foot-Washing Ritual provides a tangible connection to the love and grace that Jesus demonstrated. As you participate in this practice, reflect on how this act of service fosters a deeper understanding of forgiveness. Whether washing your own feet or those of a loved one, embrace the transformative power of humility.

Through this ritual, you honor the teachings of Christ and acknowledge the healing that comes from both giving and receiving love. Allow this experience to remind you that true forgiveness begins with an open heart, paving the way for reconciliation and growth in your relationships. Let the lessons learned during this ritual guide you on your journey toward wholeness and peace.

Your body is a temple
of the Holy Spirt.

Nourish it with care.

NOURISHING YOUR BODY AND SOUL

The human body is a remarkable network of interconnected systems, and one of the most significant relationships within it is the **gut-brain connection**. Often referred to as the "second brain," the gut houses a complex network of neurons known as the **enteric nervous system (ENS)**. This system operates independently of the brain but communicates with it through the **vagus nerve**, forming a vital link between gut health and emotional well-being.

The state of your gut health can profoundly affect your emotions. When the balance of gut bacteria is disrupted—a condition known as **dysbiosis**—it can lead to increased stress and anxiety. The gut plays a critical role in producing **serotonin**, dopamine, and other neurotransmitters, which directly impact your mood. In fact, approximately **90% of serotonin**—often called the "feel-good" neurotransmitter—is produced in the gut. This connection is essential to understanding how our digestive health influences our emotional well-being.

The Gut and Emotional Healing

Understanding the gut-brain connection sheds light on how important it is to maintain a healthy digestive system, especially when we are on a journey of forgiveness and emotional healing. Unresolved emotions like unforgiveness can manifest as stress and tension in the body, which directly impacts gut health. By nourishing your gut, you are also nurturing your emotional health, which helps in releasing negativity and promoting forgiveness.

Certain foods can actively support emotional healing and mental clarity:

- Omega-3 Fatty Acids (found in fish like salmon or plant-based sources like flaxseeds) help reduce inflammation and improve mood regulation.
- Complex Carbohydrates (whole grains, legumes, vegetables) stabilize blood sugar, supporting serotonin production and emotional balance.

NOURISHING YOUR BODY AND SOUL

- Probiotic-Rich Foods (yogurt, kefir, sauerkraut, kimchi) introduce beneficial bacteria into the gut, supporting digestion and neurotransmitter production.
- Antioxidants (berries, nuts, leafy greens) protect the brain from oxidative stress, improving cognitive function and emotional balance.

These nutrient-dense foods support the body's ability to process emotions and stress more effectively, aiding the forgiveness journey by promoting inner peace and emotional stability.

Vitamins, Minerals, and Emotional Balance

In addition to whole foods, certain **vitamins and minerals** play a key role in maintaining emotional stability. **B vitamins, vitamin D, magnesium, and zinc** are essential for neurotransmitter function and brain health.

For example:

- **Vitamin D** has been linked to reducing symptoms of depression.
- **Magnesium** helps regulate the stress response, contributing to emotional stability.

A balanced plate—containing proteins, healthy fats, and complex carbohydrates—is vital in ensuring that you are giving your body the nutrients it needs to support brain health. Regular meals and consistent hydration are also crucial in preventing mood swings and supporting mental clarity, especially when dealing with the emotional complexities of forgiveness.

NOURISHING YOUR BODY AND SOUL

Mindful Eating and Its Impact on Emotions

The practice of **mindful eating**—paying full attention to the experience of eating—can significantly improve your relationship with food and emotions. Mindful eating allows you to slow down, enjoy your meals, and reduce overeating. By focusing on how food feels and tastes, you foster a healthier relationship with what you consume, which in turn enhances your emotional and digestive health.

Hydration also plays a critical role in mood regulation. Even mild dehydration can lead to fatigue and mood disturbances. Drinking enough water throughout the day keeps your brain functioning optimally and your emotions in check.

Foods That Can Disrupt Emotional Stability

While many foods support emotional healing, some can have a negative impact on your emotional state:

- **Excessive sugar:** High sugar consumption can cause mood swings and energy crashes due to rapid fluctuations in blood glucose levels.
- **Caffeine and alcohol:** Though enjoyed by many, these substances can significantly affect emotional balance. Caffeine can increase anxiety and restlessness, while alcohol acts as a depressant, affecting sleep and mood.
- **Processed foods:** These often contain additives, preservatives, and unhealthy fats that disrupt gut health, leading to imbalances in mood and mental clarity.

Choosing whole, unprocessed foods supports a healthy gut-brain connection, which is essential in maintaining emotional balance, especially when working through difficult emotions like forgiveness.

NOURISHING YOUR BODY AND SOUL

A Foundation for Emotional Healing

The food we consume plays a crucial role not only in our physical health but also in our emotional and mental well-being. **Nourishing your body** with wholesome, nutrient-dense foods strengthens your mind's ability to cope with stress, process emotions, and navigate the challenging journey of forgiveness. A healthy gut, supported by the right foods, can lead to clearer thinking, improved mood, and greater emotional resilience, helping you work through the deep emotions tied to unforgiveness.

As we explore the powerful connection between nutrition and emotional healing, it's clear that **our bodies are intricately designed** to reflect the health of our minds. The food you choose each day can either support or hinder that process. By prioritizing foods that stabilize your mood and enhance your emotional well-being, you're giving yourself the tools to tackle the most challenging aspects of your healing journey with strength and clarity.

As you move forward, consider your diet as an essential part of your emotional and spiritual health. Taking care of your body is not separate from taking care of your soul—they are interconnected.

Healthy eating habits, along with mindful movement and prayer, provide a foundation that allows you to be more present, less weighed down by unresolved feelings, and more open to forgiveness.

As you embark on this journey, remember that nourishing your body is one of the most powerful ways to support your emotional healing, and ultimately, your forgiveness journey.

BIBLICAL PERSPECTIVES ON EATING AND FASTING

As we explore the foods and herbs mentioned in Scripture, it's essential to consider what the Bible says about eating habits and fasting. These practices hold deep significance in our physical, emotional, and spiritual well-being, offering a path toward both healing and spiritual growth.

Eating Habits in Scripture

While the Bible doesn't outline specific meal schedules, it provides valuable guidance on how we should approach food and nourishment:

Regular Nourishment:

God demonstrated the importance of consistent sustenance when He provided daily food for the Israelites.

"At twilight you shall eat meat, and in the morning you shall be filled with bread; and you shall know that I am the Lord your God." Exodus 16:12

Moderation:

Scripture warns against overindulgence, emphasizing the need for balance in our consumption.

"Do not be with heavy drinkers of wine, Or with gluttonous eaters of meat; For the heavy drinker and the glutton will come to poverty, And drowsiness will clothe one with rags." Proverbs 23:20-21

BIBLICAL PERSPECTIVES ON EATING AND FASTING

Gratitude:

We are encouraged to receive food with thankfulness, acknowledging God's provision.

"For everything created by God is good, and nothing is to be rejected if it is received with gratitude; for it is sanctified by means of the word of God and prayer." 1 Timothy 4:4-5

Fasting in the Bible

Fasting is a powerful practice in Scripture, often associated with spiritual growth, seeking God's guidance, and repentance:

Clarity:

Jesus gave specific instructions on how to fast with a pure heart, focusing on God rather than human recognition.

"But you, when you fast, anoint your head and wash your face so that your fasting will not be noticed by men, but by your Father who is in secret; and your Father who sees what is done in secret will reward you." Matthew 6:17-18

Repentance and Deliverance:

Fasting often accompanied turning back to God with a repentant heart.

"'Yet even now,' declares the Lord, 'Return to Me with all your heart, And with fasting, weeping, and mourning;'" Joel 2:12

BIBLICAL PERSPECTIVES ON EATING AND FASTING

God's Will:

The early church fasted when seeking God's direction for important decisions.

"While they were ministering to the Lord and fasting, the Holy Spirit said, 'Set apart for Me Barnabas and Saul for the work to which I have called them.'" Acts 13:2

Though the Bible doesn't explicitly list physical benefits, modern science has found that fasting may improve insulin sensitivity, support cellular repair, and promote mental clarity.

Important Safety Considerations for Fasting

While fasting can offer spiritual and potential health benefits, it's essential to approach this practice with care and wisdom. Here are some important guidelines to keep in mind:

Consult Your Healthcare Provider: Before starting any fasting regimen—especially if you have medical conditions—consult with your healthcare provider to ensure it's safe for you.

Listen to Your Body: If you feel unwell during a fast, it's important to break the fast and seek medical attention if necessary.

Stay Hydrated: Proper hydration is crucial during any fast. Most biblical fasts allowed for water, and it's wise to keep up with your daily mineral needs. A clean, healthy salt option such as Baja Gold Celtic Salt is recommended.

BIBLICAL PERSPECTIVES ON EATING AND FASTING

Start Slowly: If you're new to fasting, begin with shorter fasting periods and gradually increase the duration as your body adjusts.

Maintain Balanced Nutrition: When not fasting, focus on a balanced diet that supports your overall health and well-being.

Spiritual Focus: In the biblical context, fasting is primarily about drawing closer to God, not weight loss or physical benefits. Always keep your spiritual intentions at the forefront.

Fasting as Part of the Forgiveness Journey

As we walk through the path of forgiveness and healing, practices like mindful eating and periodic fasting can play a key role in supporting spiritual growth. Fasting offers an opportunity to turn our hearts toward God, seeking His wisdom and strength in moments of emotional release and healing.

Remember, **our goal is holistic well-being and mental clarity**—caring for our bodies as temples of the Holy Spirit while nurturing our souls by deepening our relationship with God. When approached thoughtfully and with prayer, fasting can be a powerful practice for both spiritual renewal and emotional restoration.

ANCIENT WISDOM, MODERN HEALING

As we walk the path of forgiveness and healing, it's enlightening to look back at the ancient wisdom preserved in the Scriptures. The Bible, beyond its profound spiritual teachings, offers practical knowledge about health and healing through the foods and herbs mentioned throughout its pages. These elements, used for nourishment, healing, and even symbolic purposes, offer insights into both physical and emotional well-being.

Throughout Scripture, we encounter powerful substances: **the soothing balm of Gilead, the preservative power of salt, the sweetness of honey, and the bitterness of wormwood.** Each of these carries significant meaning, both in terms of their health benefits and their deeper, metaphorical resonance. As we explore these ancient remedies, we'll see how they can inform our modern understanding of holistic health, and offer rich metaphors for our journey toward forgiveness and emotional healing.

Ancient Healing, Modern Application

While we'll be examining these foods and herbs through a biblical lens, it's important to note that this is not an invitation to replace modern medicine. Rather, we are invited to appreciate the wisdom of our ancestors and the cultural and historical context of biblical healing practices. These insights provide a bridge between ancient wisdom and our modern pursuit of wholeness—physically, emotionally, and spiritually.

Each biblical food and herb holds a dual purpose: offering practical benefits while also shedding light on spiritual truths.

For example, bitter herbs remind us of the necessity to confront and process our pain, while the healing properties of plants like aloe mirror God's power to restore and renew. The preservative nature of salt points us to the enduring and unchanging nature of God's covenant love, a constant reminder of His presence throughout our healing process.

ANCIENT WISDOM, MODERN HEALING

A Journey Through Biblical Remedies

In the following pages, we'll explore a variety of foods and herbs mentioned in the Bible, each with its own unique history, benefits, and symbolism. We'll uncover how these ancient remedies can enlighten our path to emotional and spiritual healing:

- **The Balm of Gilead**, referenced for its soothing qualities, can remind us of God's comfort in times of pain.
- **Honey**, often associated with abundance and blessing, can symbolize the sweetness of healing and restoration after forgiveness.
- **Wormwood**, bitter and unpleasant, teaches us that confronting bitterness is an essential step toward growth and peace.
- **Salt**, essential for preserving and flavoring, is a symbol of God's enduring love and faithfulness, preserving our souls as we navigate the challenges of life.

Holistic Healing: Body, Mind, and Spirit

As we delve into the physical and symbolic aspects of these biblical elements, may we not only learn how to support our physical health but also nourish our spirits. God, in His wisdom, provided for both our bodies and souls, and through these remedies, we are reminded of His care and provision in every aspect of our lives.

Let us reflect on Proverbs 17:22, which tells us, *"A joyful heart is good medicine, But a broken spirit dries up the bones."*

In exploring the ancient wisdom of these foods and herbs, may we also remember that joy, peace, and forgiveness are essential to our healing journey. As we work toward releasing the burdens of the past and our lives, may we embrace both the physical and spiritual nourishment that God offers.

FOODS THAT SUPPORT EMOTIONAL HEALING

The connection between what we eat and how we feel emotionally is profound. Our diet plays a crucial role in supporting mental and emotional well-being, and certain foods can help stabilize mood, reduce anxiety, and promote healing.

Omega-3 Fatty Acids and Mood Regulation

Omega-3 fatty acids are essential for brain health and mood regulation. Found in fish like salmon and plant-based sources like flaxseeds, they help reduce inflammation and promote the production of anti-inflammatory molecules, which can alleviate symptoms of depression and anxiety. Incorporating omega-3s into your diet is a powerful way to support emotional well-being and reduce mental stress.

The Importance of Complex Carbohydrates for Serotonin Production

Complex carbohydrates, such as whole grains, legumes, and vegetables, play a vital role in serotonin production. Serotonin is a neurotransmitter that helps regulate mood, and by consuming complex carbs, you can help stabilize blood sugar levels, which in turn promotes a more balanced emotional state. The steady release of glucose from these foods enhances feelings of contentment and well-being, making them an essential part of an emotionally healthy diet.

Probiotic-Rich Foods for Gut Health

The health of your gut is directly connected to your mental health, thanks to the gut-brain axis. Probiotic-rich foods like yogurt, kefir, sauerkraut, and kimchi help maintain a healthy gut microbiome. These foods introduce beneficial bacteria into the gut, which supports digestion, reduces inflammation, and positively impacts mental health by producing neurotransmitters that influence your emotional state.

FOODS THAT SUPPORT EMOTIONAL HEALING

Antioxidants and Their Impact on Brain Health

Antioxidants are powerful compounds found in foods like berries, nuts, and leafy greens. They protect the brain from oxidative stress, a process that can damage brain cells and contribute to mental health disorders. By neutralizing free radicals, antioxidants improve cognitive function and emotional balance. A diet rich in antioxidants helps maintain mental clarity and emotional resilience, key elements for overall well-being.

Vitamins and Minerals Crucial for Emotional Balance

Certain vitamins and minerals play an essential role in supporting emotional health. Key nutrients include B vitamins, vitamin D, magnesium, and zinc. These nutrients are vital for neurotransmitter function, energy production, and brain health:

- B Vitamins help regulate mood and reduce feelings of anxiety and depression.
- Vitamin D has been linked to improved mood and reduced symptoms of depression, especially in individuals with low levels.
- Magnesium supports the regulation of stress responses, promoting calmness.
- Zinc helps with brain function and mood regulation, supporting emotional balance.

Incorporating foods rich in these nutrients—such as leafy greens, nuts, seeds, and fortified dairy products—can enhance your mental and emotional health.

BIBLICAL FOODS AND HEALING IN SCRIPTURE

The Bible offers wisdom about foods and herbs used for nourishment and healing, reflecting the deep connection between physical and emotional health.

These foods, which were essential for both daily sustenance and symbolic significance in biblical times, also serve as metaphors for healing and restoration in our lives today.

Olive Oil

Benefits: Healing wounds, skincare, and anointing.
Usage: Applied topically or used in cooking.

"And came to him and bandaged up his wounds, pouring oil and wine on them." Luke 10:34

Wine

Benefits: Disinfectant and medicinal purposes.
Usage: Consumed in moderation or applied topically.

"No longer drink water exclusively, but use a little wine for the sake of your stomach and your frequent ailments." 1 Timothy 5:23

Hyssop

Benefits: Used for purification, often as an antibiotic in cleansing rituals.
Usage: Often involved in spiritual purification.

"Purify me with hyssop, and I shall be clean; Wash me, and I shall be whiter than snow." Psalm 51:7

BIBLICAL FOODS AND HEALING IN SCRIPTURE

Balm of Gilead

Benefits: Healing wounds and soothing pain.
Usage: Applied topically.

"Is there no balm in Gilead? Is there no physician there? Why then has not the health of the daughter of my people been restored?" Jeremiah 8:22

Garlic, Onions, and Leeks

Benefits: General health, anti-inflammatory properties, and flavor.
Usage: Consumed as food.

"We remember the fish which we used to eat free in Egypt, the cucumbers and the melons and the leeks and the onions and the garlic." Numbers 11:5

Mint, Cumin, and Dill

Benefits: Aids digestion and adds flavor.
Usage: Used in cooking and possibly medicinally.

"Does he not level its surface And sow dill and scatter cumin And plant wheat in rows, Barley in its place and rye within its area?" Isaiah 28:25

Spikenard

Benefits: Aromatic oil used for anointing.
Usage: In perfumes and for anointing.

"While He was in Bethany at the home of Simon the leper, a woman came with an alabaster vial of costly perfume and poured it over His head."
Mark 14:3

BIBLICAL FOODS AND HEALING IN SCRIPTURE

Mustard Seed

Benefits: Used medicinally and as a spice; symbolizes faith.
Usage: In cooking and metaphorically.

"And He *said to them, "Because of the littleness of your faith; for truly I say to you, if you have faith the size of a mustard seed, you will say to this mountain, 'Move from here to there,' and it will move; and nothing will be impossible to you."" Matthew 17:20

Cinnamon and Cassia

Benefits: Aromatic spices used in anointing oil.
Usage: In perfumes and anointing oils.

"Take also for yourself the finest of spices: of flowing myrrh five hundred shekels, and of fragrant cinnamon half as much, two hundred and fifty, and of fragrant cane two hundred and fifty, and of cassia five hundred, according to the shekel of the sanctuary, and of olive oil a hin." Exodus 30:23-24

It's important to remember that while these foods and herbs were mentioned in the Bible for their healing and nourishing properties, their usage today should be guided by modern medical knowledge.

The Bible's references often carry symbolic or cultural significance beyond their physical properties.

Always consult with healthcare professionals before using any herbs or foods for medicinal purposes, but trust in the wisdom passed down through the ages.

SALT: A SYMBOL OF FORGIVENESS AND HEALING

Salt holds multifaceted properties and offers a powerful metaphor for the forgiveness journey. Just as salt preserves, purifies, and enhances flavor, forgiveness can play similar roles in our lives and relationships.

Preservation

Forgiveness acts as a spiritual and emotional preservative, safeguarding our hearts from the corrosive effects of bitterness and resentment. Like salt preserving food, forgiveness preserves the goodness in our lives, preventing the decay that unforgiveness often brings.

Purification

Salt was used in biblical purification rituals. Similarly, forgiveness purifies our hearts and minds, cleansing us from the toxic effects of holding onto past hurts, enabling us to view others and ourselves through a lens of grace.

Enhancement

Just as salt enhances the flavor of food, forgiveness enhances the quality of our life experiences. It deepens our empathy, strengthens our resilience, and adds depth to our character.

Covenant

In Scripture, salt symbolized the permanence and purity of God's covenant. In a similar way, forgiveness can be viewed as a covenant we make with ourselves, others, and God. It represents a commitment to choose love over resentment and reconciliation over division.

Salt was highly valued for its preservative and symbolic properties, representing purity, loyalty, and God's covenant.

SALT: A SYMBOL OF FORGIVENESS AND HEALING

Salt is a powerful symbol in the Bible, representing preservation, purification, and covenant. It was used not only to season food but also in sacred rituals and offerings, highlighting its spiritual significance. As we explore these scriptures, we see how salt serves as a metaphor for the enduring quality of God's covenant, the transformative power of forgiveness, and the call for us to be a purifying influence in the world.

Just as salt enhances and preserves, these scriptures remind us of our role in upholding faith, preserving peace, and extending forgiveness in our relationships.

"Every grain offering of yours, moreover, you shall season with salt, so that the salt of the covenant of your God shall not be lacking from your grain offering; with all your offerings you shall offer salt." Leviticus 2:13

"He went out to the spring of water and threw salt in it and said, 'Thus says the Lord, I have purified these waters; there shall not be from there death or unfruitfulness any longer.'" 2 Kings 2:21

"You are the salt of the earth; but if the salt has become tasteless, how can it be made salty again? It is no longer good for anything, except to be thrown out and trampled underfoot by men." Matthew 5:13

By exploring these ancient biblical foods and herbs, we gain not only practical insights into their physical uses but also profound spiritual metaphors.

> **Salt has a distinct quality that can't be replicated. This teaches that Christians should maintain their distinct character and not lose their "saltiness" by conforming to worldly values.**

WORMWOOD: A METAPHOR FOR BITTERNESS AND HEALING

Wormwood, with its potent bitterness, serves as a profound metaphor in the forgiveness journey. **Much like its overwhelming flavor, resentment and unforgiveness can dominate our emotional and spiritual well-being, casting a shadow over our lives and relationships.** The scriptures reference wormwood as a symbol of judgment, sorrow, and bitterness, reflecting the internal consequences of holding onto past hurts.

Bitterness
Wormwood represents the bitterness that can grow in our hearts when we hold onto anger and resentment. Just as wormwood overwhelms the palate, unforgiveness can overwhelm our emotional landscape, clouding our perspectives and tainting our interactions with others. Forgiveness, on the other hand, allows us to uproot this bitterness, freeing ourselves from its corrosive grip.

Consequences
In the Bible, wormwood often symbolizes the painful consequences of sin and turning away from God. Holding onto unforgiveness can have similar far-reaching effects, impacting our mental, emotional, and spiritual health. By recognizing the bitterness within us, we can begin the process of healing, addressing the root causes of our pain, and inviting God's grace to restore us.

Healing
While wormwood is a symbol of bitterness, it also serves as a medicinal herb with healing properties. In the same way, forgiveness has the power to heal our wounded hearts and relationships. Just as wormwood's bitterness can be used for purification, forgiving others helps purify our hearts from the burdens of anger and resentment, leading to renewed peace and inner freedom.

WORMWOOD: A METAPHOR FOR BITTERNESS AND HEALING

Transformation

Choosing to confront the bitterness represented by wormwood allows us to transform our hearts and lives. When we release the acrid taste of resentment, we make room for forgiveness to bring sweetness and healing into our experiences. This transformation mirrors the power of God's grace, turning bitterness into blessing.

Wormwood is frequently mentioned in Scripture as a symbol of bitterness and judgment, illustrating the spiritual consequences of withholding forgiveness. As we explore these verses, we are reminded of the importance of addressing the bitterness in our hearts and replacing it with the healing and peace that comes through forgiveness.

"But in the end she is bitter as wormwood, Sharp as a two-edged sword."
Proverbs 5:4

"Therefore thus says the Lord of hosts, the God of Israel, 'Behold, I will feed them, this people, with wormwood and give them poisoned water to drink.'"
Jeremiah 9:15

"The name of the star is called Wormwood; and a third of the waters became wormwood, and many men died from the waters, because they were made bitter." Revelation 8:11

By reflecting on these biblical references, we can see the powerful lesson that wormwood offers: bitterness, left unchecked, can have far-reaching consequences.

But through forgiveness, we can transform our hearts, releasing bitterness and embracing the sweetness of God's grace.

PRACTICING MINDFUL EATING AND MODERATION

The Bible provides wisdom on moderation and self-control, both of which are essential for maintaining emotional well-being.

While it doesn't explicitly categorize foods as "good" or "bad," it offers principles that, combined with modern nutritional science, can guide us in making choices that support our mental and emotional health.

Let's explore some foods and substances that may negatively impact our emotional well-being when consumed in excess.

Excessive Sugar

High sugar intake causes rapid blood sugar fluctuations, which can lead to mood swings, irritability, and fatigue. It's important to be mindful of sugar consumption to maintain emotional balance.

"Have you found honey? Eat only what you need, That you not have it in excess and vomit it." Proverbs 25:16

Alcohol

While moderate alcohol consumption may have some benefits, excessive drinking can disrupt sleep patterns, increase anxiety and depression, and impair judgment. Limiting alcohol can help promote emotional stability and better mental health.

"Wine is a mocker, strong drink a brawler, And whoever is intoxicated by it is not wise." Proverbs 20:1

PRACTICING MINDFUL EATING AND MODERATION

Caffeine

While caffeine can provide a temporary boost, excessive intake can lead to heightened anxiety, sleep disturbances, dehydration and increased stress responses. Moderating caffeine consumption is key to maintaining emotional well-being.

"All things are lawful for me, but not all things are profitable. All things are lawful for me, but I will not be mastered by anything." 1 Corinthians 6:12

Processed Foods

Highly processed foods often lack essential nutrients and can contribute to inflammation, which affects both mood and cognitive function. Reducing processed foods and replacing them with nutrient-dense options can improve emotional health.

"When you sit down to dine with a ruler, Consider carefully what is before you, And put a knife to your throat If you are a man of great appetite. Do not desire his delicacies, For it is deceptive food." Proverbs 23:1-3

Trans Fats

Trans fats have been linked to an increased risk of depression and can negatively impact brain health. Avoiding trans fats and opting for healthier fats, such as those found in olive oil or avocados, supports better emotional and mental well-being.

"For you have been bought with a price: therefore glorify God in your body." 1 Corinthians 6:20

PRACTICING MINDFUL EATING AND MODERATION

Artificial Sweeteners

Some studies suggest that artificial sweeteners may affect gut bacteria, which in turn could influence mood and behavior. While more research is needed, it's a good practice to limit artificial sweeteners and prioritize natural alternatives.

"How sweet are Your words to my taste! Yes, sweeter than honey to my mouth!" Psalm 119:103

While it's important to be mindful of these potentially problematic foods, the Bible emphasizes balance and gratitude in our eating habits rather than strict prohibitions. As Paul writes, "Therefore, whether you eat or drink, or whatever you do, do all to the glory of God." 1 Corinthians 10:31

Here are some practical steps you can take to support emotional well-being through mindful eating:

- Practice mindful eating: Pay attention to how different foods affect your mood and energy levels
- Reduce processed foods: Gradually replace them with whole, nutrient-dense options that nourish both your body and mind.
- Monitor caffeine and alcohol consumption: Be aware of how these substances affect your emotional health, especially if you struggle with anxiety or sleep disturbances.
- Balance indulgences: Occasional treats are part of a balanced life. Focus on overall healthy eating patterns, not perfection.
- Express gratitude: Approach your diet with gratitude, recognizing all food as a gift from God to be enjoyed in moderation.

Writing brings clarity to the heart's deepest thoughts.

THE POWER OF JOURNALING

Journaling is more than just putting words on paper; it's a powerful tool for self-discovery, emotional release, and spiritual growth. When we are on a journey of forgiveness, the act of writing can help us process the deep and often complex emotions that accompany hurt and pain. Through journaling, we give ourselves permission to slow down, reflect, and explore what's truly happening within us—things we might not be able to articulate out loud.

At its core, journaling is an act of honesty. It's a space where we can be entirely real with ourselves and with God. No judgment, no filters—just raw thoughts and emotions as they come. Whether you are working through forgiving someone else, or perhaps even forgiving yourself, journaling can be the place where you start to uncover truths and gain new perspectives. It allows you to face the difficult emotions head-on, to sit with them, and to begin the process of healing and release.

For many, the path to forgiveness is not straightforward. It involves layers of hurt, misunderstandings, and lingering resentment. By journaling, we begin to peel back those layers, finding the underlying reasons why forgiveness might feel so hard. It helps us notice patterns in our thinking, reflect on how we've been carrying emotional burdens, and perhaps most importantly, it offers a space for prayerful introspection. When we invite God into this process, journaling becomes a spiritual practice, helping us discern His guidance and wisdom as we move toward a place of peace.

The benefits of journaling extend beyond emotional and spiritual wellness. Research shows that journaling can reduce stress, boost mood, and even improve physical health by strengthening the mind-body connection. When we take time to write, we are giving ourselves a moment to pause and breathe, allowing the brain to process emotions and experiences in a way that brings greater clarity.

THE POWER OF JOURNALING

In the context of forgiveness, journaling serves as a personal witness to your journey. Each entry marks progress, no matter how small. It creates a tangible record of your growth, your struggles, and ultimately, your healing. Some days, the words may flow easily, while other days may feel more difficult—but each moment you spend journaling is a step toward wholeness.

As you begin this journaling process, remember that there is no right or wrong way to do it. This is your space to reflect, release, and grow. Whether you're documenting emotions, praying through words, or writing letters to yourself and others, let journaling be a companion on your journey toward forgiveness and emotional freedom. Trust that with time, your words will become a bridge to deeper understanding, healing, and connection with God.

Let your pen move freely, knowing that each word brings you closer to healing, clarity, peace and most importantly helps you create a stronger connection to Abba (God).

UNLOCKING HEALING THROUGH JOURNALING

Before diving into the journaling exercises, take a moment to reflect on the purpose of these activities. Journaling provides a safe, private space to process emotions, release burdens, and gain clarity on the forgiveness journey.

As you explore the following exercises, remember that this practice is for you and God, allowing your thoughts to flow freely without judgment or expectation. Each activity is designed to help you uncover insights, release pain, and invite healing into your heart and mind.

Tips for Journaling:

- Start small: Even if you only have 5 minutes, start with what feels manageable.
- Choose a consistent time: Find a moment in your day that works best—whether in the morning or before bed
- Use prompts: If you're unsure of what to write, forgiveness-related prompts can guide you.

Emotional Release Writing

Set a timer for 15 minutes and write freely about a situation you're struggling to forgive. Don't focus on structure or grammar; let your emotions flow onto the page. When you're done, take a deep breath and reflect on how you feel. This practice can help release built-up tension and bring clarity.

Scriptural Journaling

Choose a Bible verse on forgiveness, like Colossians 3:13 or Ephesians 4:32. Write it at the top of your journal page, and then reflect on how the verse applies to your situation. End with a prayer asking the Lord to connect this verse to your life and see how he speaks to you.

UNLOCKING HEALING THROUGH JOURNALING

Daily Reflection

For a week, take time each day to reflect and write:

- What emotions am I experiencing about the situation I'm working to forgive?
- How have these emotions affected my actions today?
- Did I live within my integrity?
- Am I starting to live as a person who quickly forgives offenses?

Gratitude Journaling for Healing

Gratitude can shift our focus from hurt to healing. For the next five days, write down:

- Three things you're grateful for, no matter how small.
- One positive quality or lesson you've developed through your challenging experience.
- A short prayer thanking God for His presence in your journey.

Reflection on Emotions

Pick a situation that's difficult to forgive and write about the emotions it stirs. Go back to the feelings wheel and expand your emotional vocabulary. Have you become more aware of the depth of feelings God has given us? If so, which ones?

UNLOCKING HEALING THROUGH JOURNALING

Creating Distance from Negative Thoughts

Identify any recurring negative thought that surfaces during your forgiveness journey. When this thought comes to mind, take a moment to observe how it makes you feel. Bring the thought into the light and ask yourself: does this thought truly reflect what is real? Or is there a truth from God's Word that directly counters it? If so, write down that truth as a reminder. By holding your thoughts up to His promises, you allow His perspective to bring clarity and renewal.

Moments of Strength

Reflect on three recent moments where you demonstrated strength, patience, or compassion—attributes God has instilled within you. Describe each experience and consider how God's presence empowered you to respond as you did. Let these reflections remind you that His strength is alive in you, guiding and equipping you on your journey toward forgiveness.

After trying these exercises, take a moment to reflect on your journaling experience. Has it helped you in your forgiveness process? Set a personal goal for how you'll continue incorporating journaling over the next week.

WORDS OF HOPE AND HEALING

Journaling, like forgiveness, is a journey—one that unfolds uniquely for each individual. Some days, the words may flow easily, capturing the emotions that surface as you write. On other days, you might struggle to find the right expression, feeling the weight of unprocessed feelings or unresolved thoughts. In these moments, be gentle with yourself. Allow the words to come as they may, knowing that every entry is valid and important.

This practice is a sacred dialogue between you and God—a private space for honesty, exploration, and revelation. There's no right or wrong way to journal; what matters is the intention behind your writing and the openness of your heart. Trust the process, even when it feels challenging.

"For I know the plans that I have for you," declares the Lord, *"plans for welfare and not for calamity to give you a future and a hope."* (Jeremiah 29:11)

This promise is a reminder that God holds a vision for your life that is filled with hope, healing, and purpose.

Embrace the journey of journaling as a vital part of your path to emotional freedom and connection with our Heavenly Father. Let it be a source of encouragement, reflection, and prayer as you navigate God's plan for you. Through this practice, may you come to live in the peace and grace that flows from choosing a life of forgiveness.

May these moments of journaling become a sacred meeting place with the Father, Jesus, and the Holy Spirit—a space for intimate connection and open-hearted dialogue where you can share, listen, and experience the fullness of His love and guidance in a bidirectional way.

BONUS MATERIALS

Continuing Your Journey

The following pages are blank worksheets provided for you to continue practicing the exercises and activities introduced throughout this workbook. Feel free to scan or duplicate these pages as needed for your personal reflection and growth.

Please note, these worksheets are intended for personal use only. Duplication, distribution, or recreation of these materials for commercial purposes or any unauthorized use is strictly prohibited. May these pages support you on your ongoing journey toward healing, forgiveness, and spiritual growth.

WRITE YOUR LETTER TO JESUS

Write your letter to Jesus, as your friend and comforter, sharing what you need in a best friend. He's ready to listen whenever you're ready to share.

Dear Jesus,

FORGIVENESS INVENTORY

Create a list of people, organizations, and situations that trigger feelings of offense or resentment within you. Ensuring a comprehensive inventory is crucial.

CREATE YOUR PSALM TO GOD

Selah

SHARING YOUR GRIEF WITH GOD

Some grief must be shared to be healed. Take this time to write a letter to our Heavenly Father, pouring out your sorrow and burdens. Share your pain with Him and allow Jesus, your Comforter, to walk with you through your healing.

A LETTER OF COMPASSION

EXPLORING FORGIVENESS

Now, choose one person from your list for our first detailed exploration.

Delve into the specifics: What did they do? How did they hurt you?

Be specific and thorough. This is your opportunity to express everything, leaving no room for unresolved feelings or negative influences to linger or strongholds to take effect.

WHAT DO YOU FEEL YOU ARE OWED?

IDENTIFY THE PAIN

Every offense stems from a hurt: Circle or highlight the emotions that you feel best describe the pain you've experienced.

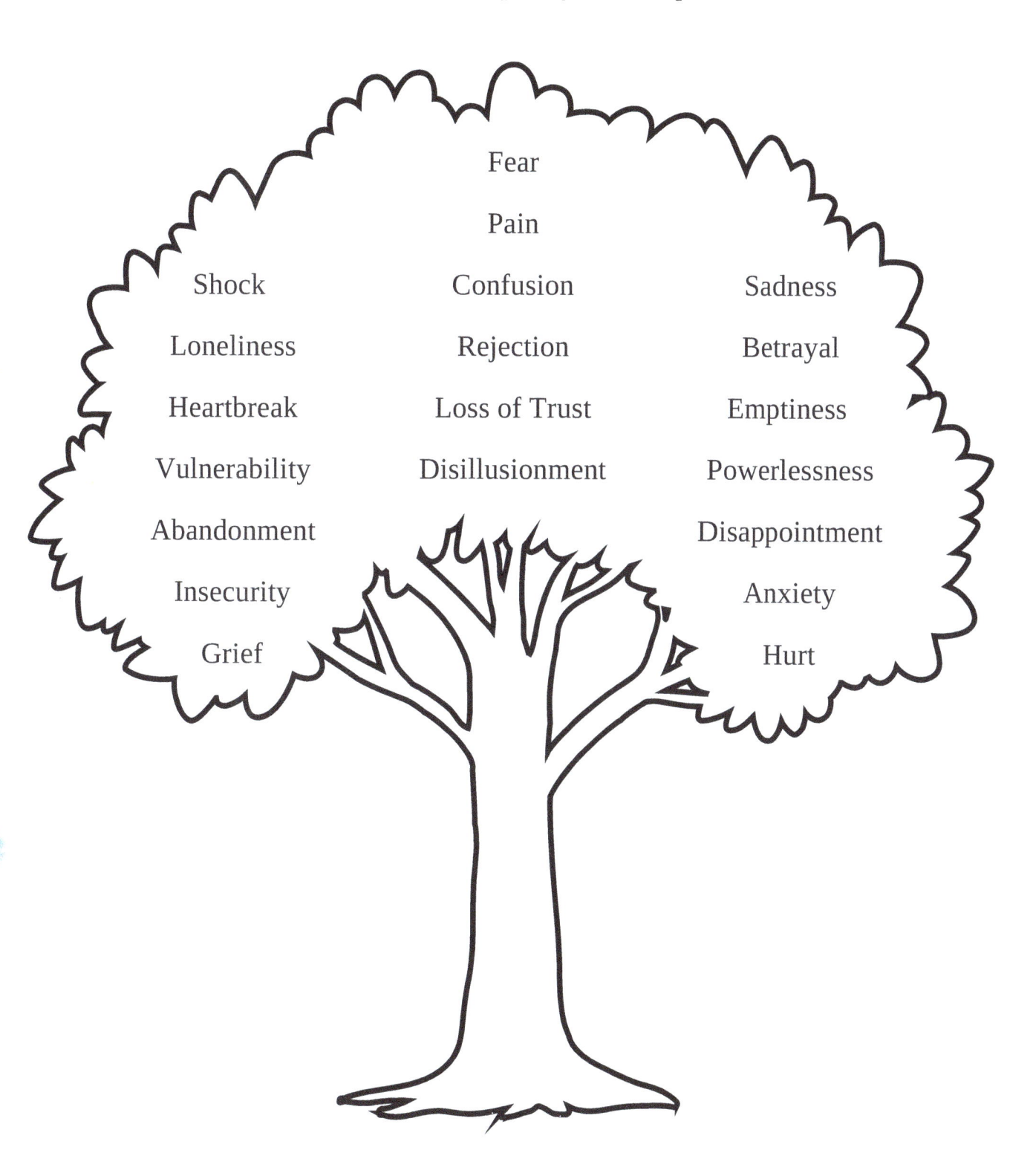

Fear

Pain

Shock Confusion Sadness

Loneliness Rejection Betrayal

Heartbreak Loss of Trust Emptiness

Vulnerability Disillusionment Powerlessness

Abandonment Disappointment

Insecurity Anxiety

Grief Hurt

IDENTIFYING HARMFUL LABELS

As you read through this list of examples, take a moment to listen to your heart and see if any of these resonate with you. These labels, often picked up through negative self-talk, hurtful words from others, or societal stereotypes, may have shaped how you see yourself.

Unworthy	Useless	Invisible
Failure	Burden	Annoying
Unlovable	Irresponsible	Problematic
Weak	Unwanted	Defective
Stupid	Disappointing	Worthless
Broken	Pathetic	Dumb
Ugly	Coward	Inferior
Lazy	Insecure	Unsuccessful
Not Good Enough	Loser	Damaged

CONFRONTING NEGATIVE LABELS

Now it's time to reflect on the labels we've taken on—whether they've come from our own negative self-talk, the hurtful words of others, or stereotypes that have been imposed upon us. These labels, along with the harmful words we often speak over ourselves, can shape how we see our worth. Let's take a moment to recognize them so we can begin the journey of releasing their hold.

Step 1: Identify the Labels
Reflect on the negative labels you've internalized. Take a moment to consider the labels that have come from your own negative self-talk, those given by people who hurt or bullied you, and stereotypes that may have been imposed on you. As you think through this, refer back to the list of examples and identify any that resonate with your experience.

Step 2: Write Down Each Label
List each label on a separate line. Be specific and honest about the labels you have carried.

CONFRONTING NEGATIVE LABELS

Step 3: Reflect on the Impact
For each label, write a few sentences about how it has affected your self-esteem, behavior, and choices. Consider how these labels have shaped your self-perception and interactions with others.

_____
_____
_____
_____
_____
_____
_____
_____

Step 4: Challenge the Labels
Identify any evidence that contradicts each label. Write down positive attributes or achievements that disprove the negative labels.

_____
_____
_____
_____
_____
_____
_____
_____

CONFRONTING NEGATIVE LABELS

Step 5: Letting Go
For each label, write a statement of release, affirming your decision to let go of the negative label. Replace it with a positive affirmation or a more accurate description of yourself.

Example:

Label: "Unworthy"
Impact: This label has made me doubt my value and hesitate to pursue opportunities.
Contradiction: I have received praise for my work and have strong relationships that affirm my worth.
Release Statement: I release the label "unworthy" and affirm that I am valuable and deserving of success. By working through this exercise, you can begin to shed the negative labels that have held you back and embrace a more positive and accurate self-image.

CONFRONTING NEGATIVE LABELS

Step 5: Letting Go - Continued

PRACTICE SELF-FORGIVENESS

To identify areas where you're holding onto shame, accept God's forgiveness, and practice self-forgiveness.

<u>Step 1: Identify an Instance of Shame, Regret or Self Condemnation</u>
List 3-5 past actions or decisions that you're still holding onto shame about. For each, write down:
a) What happened
b) Why you feel ashamed
c) How this shame is affecting your life now

PRACTICE SELF-FORGIVENESS

Step 2: List the Consequences

List the negative consequences you have experienced as a result of not forgiving yourself. Consider how these consequences have impacted your mental health, relationships, and overall well-being. Then bring it to God.

_____
_____
_____
_____
_____
_____

Step 3: Acknowledge God's Forgiveness

For each item on your list, write out or meditate on this truth: "God has forgiven me for this through Jesus Christ." (*You might find it helpful to write out 1 John 1:9 personalized to your situation.*)

_____
_____
_____
_____
_____
_____
_____
_____
_____

PRACTICE SELF-FORGIVENESS

Step 4: Release the Shame

For each item, write a statement of self-forgiveness. For example: "As I am already forgiven, I forgive myself for [action]. I choose to release this and accept God's forgiveness and love."

Step 5: Positive Affirmation

Write a positive affirmation or truth to counter each shame-based thought. For example, if you feel "I'm unworthy," your affirmation might be "I am worthy of love and belonging because God loves me unconditionally."

PRACTICE SELF-FORGIVENESS

Step 6: Moving Forward

For each situation, write down one lesson you've learned and one way you can use this experience to grow or help others.

PRACTICE SELF-FORGIVENESS

Step 7: Reinforce and Embrace
Choose one of your affirmations or a relevant Bible verse to meditate on daily for the next week. This will help reinforce your decision to embrace self-forgiveness.

_____

_____

_____

_____

_____

_____

_____

_____

Remember, self-forgiveness is a process. It will take time and repeated effort to fully release shame and embrace God's forgiveness. Be patient with yourself. As you practice self-forgiveness, you'll likely experience greater peace, improved relationships, and a closer connection with God.

By accepting forgiveness — both from God and yourself — you open the door to healing and growth. You free yourself from the burden of shame and create space for positive experiences and deeper spiritual connection.

Remember, you are worthy of forgiveness and love, not because of what you do or don't do, but because of who you are: **a beloved child of God.**

A PRAYER FOR GUIDANCE

Take a moment to write a heartfelt prayer or letter to God. Express your gratitude for His forgiveness and ask for His guidance and strength as you continue on the journey of forgiving yourself.

Selah

CONNECTING WITH LONG-SUFFERING IN YOUR JOURNEY

Long-suffering doesn't just shape our relationships with others; it also transforms our relationship with God. It deepens our faith, builds endurance, and ultimately aligns our hearts with the eternal love and patience that Jesus has for each of us. As we experience long-suffering, we are being shaped into His likeness, and our ability to love grows stronger with each challenge.

As you explore the concept of long-suffering, consider these reflective questions to help deepen your understanding and apply this lesson to your own experiences.

Think about a time when you've had to endure a difficult situation with patience and love. How did that experience shape your heart and your relationship with others?

_____
_____
_____

In what ways can you invite Jesus to help you practice long-suffering in your current relationships, especially when it's hard to forgive or be patient?

_____
_____
_____

How has embracing the concept of long-suffering deepened your faith and brought you closer to understanding the love Christ has for you?

_____
_____
_____

CREATE YOUR FORGIVENESS JELLYFISH

UNCOVERING HIDDEN HURT AND UNFORGIVENESS

Sometimes, the hurts we've experienced throughout our lives remain hidden beneath the surface, buried so deep that we may not even realize they're still affecting us. These unresolved feelings of unforgiveness can impact our emotions, relationships, and sense of peace. This activity is designed to help you take a closer look at your life, identify any hidden hurts, and begin the process of letting go.

By creating a historical timeline, you'll be able to map out different stages of your life and reflect on events that may still carry emotional weight. This exercise will help you identify areas where unforgiveness might be lingering and guide you in working toward healing and freedom.

Step 1: Identify Significant Life Stages

Start by listing major periods in your life. Think of distinct phases such as childhood, high school, college, work, or different relationships. These stages will help you organize your reflections. If you experienced challenges like being bullied at school, work, or home, consider these as potential starting points. Write them out below.

UNCOVERING HIDDEN HURT AND UNFORGIVENESS

Step 2: Choose One Life Stage and Map a Timeline

From the life stages you've listed, choose one that feels particularly significant or unresolved. Create a timeline for this stage, focusing on the sequence of events. Start by mapping what led up to the experience, the key events that defined it, and what happened afterward. This will help you uncover patterns and the ripple effects of that time in your life, allowing you to better understand how this specific stage shaped your emotional journey.

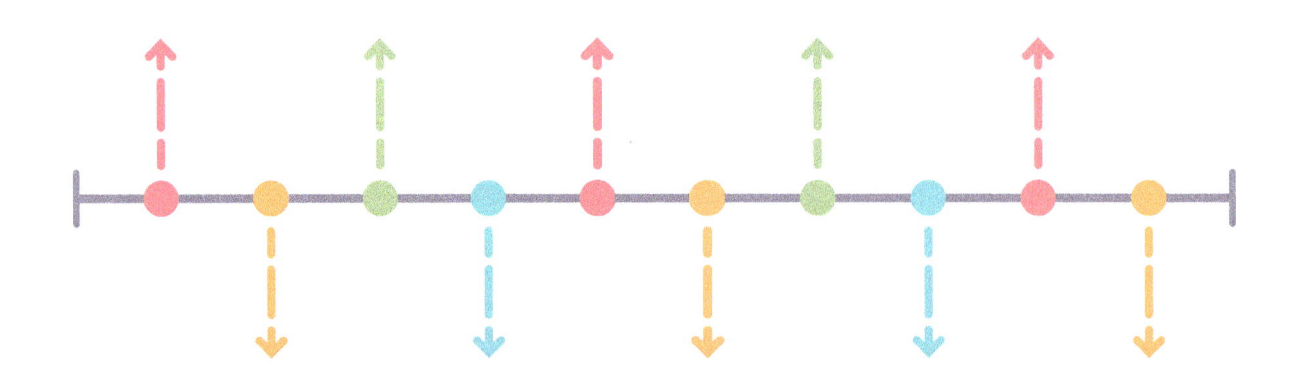

UNCOVERING HIDDEN HURT AND UNFORGIVENESS

Step 3: Reflect on the Positive and Negative Aspects

Take time to reflect on the key moments that stand out. Consider both the positive and negative aspects of this stage, focusing on the events that had the most emotional impact. Identify which experiences brought growth and joy, and which left emotional scars. This reflection will help you gain a deeper understanding of how this period influenced your personal and spiritual development.

UNCOVERING HIDDEN HURT AND UNFORGIVENESS

Step 4: Note Down Painful Experiences

As you reflect on this specific life stage, take note of any painful or challenging experiences that stand out. This could include moments of betrayal, unfair treatment, personal disappointments, or times when you felt deeply hurt. The goal is to pinpoint the events that left lasting emotional wounds, helping you recognize the areas in need of healing from Jesus.

UNCOVERING HIDDEN HURT AND UNFORGIVENESS

Step 5: Assess Your Emotional Response

For each experience you've listed, think about how it makes you feel now. Do you still feel anger, resentment, or hurt when you remember these events? Write these feelings down. This step will help you gauge your current emotional response and identify lingering pain.

_____
_____
_____
_____
_____
_____

Step 6: Identify Areas of Unforgiveness

If any of the experiences still stir up strong negative emotions, it may indicate that there's lingering unforgiveness. Identify both people and events tied to these unresolved feelings. Write them down—people will be added to your forgiveness inventory for individual forgiveness worksheets, while events can be further explored using the Forgiveness Jellyfish exercise to work through the deeper emotional impact.

_____   _____
_____   _____
_____   _____
_____   _____

UNCOVERING HIDDEN HURT AND UNFORGIVENESS

Step 7: Look for Lessons and Blessings

Part of the forgiveness process is recognizing the lessons and blessings that may have come out of difficult times. Even in the midst of hardship, there can be moments of growth, wisdom, or unexpected blessings. Reflect on how these painful experiences have shaped you and what you may have learned. Keep a note of these for future moments of gratitude.

_____
_____
_____
_____
_____
_____
_____
_____
_____

Step 8: Revisit and Expand Your Journey

At your own pace, return to the list of significant life stages you originally created. Take the time to work through this entire exercise for each stage that you feel may hold hidden hurt or unresolved unforgiveness. Healing is a process, and as you grow, new insights may emerge. Regularly review your progress, update your timeline, and prioritize forgiving both others and yourself as you uncover these areas. This ongoing reflection will help you continue releasing burdens and moving forward with emotional and spiritual freedom.

RESTORING THROUGH APOLOGY

Now that you've reflected on who may be in need of your apology—whether it's another person or yourself—take a moment to apply the steps you just learned. Craft a sincere apology by owning your actions, expressing genuine regret, and showing understanding for the impact of your behavior. Consider how you can make amends and ask for forgiveness with humility and grace.

Whether this apology is one you plan to deliver to someone else or a way to offer forgiveness to yourself, take the time to write it thoughtfully and from the heart.

Step 1: Own It

_____
_____
_____
_____
_____
_____

Step 2: Express Regret

_____
_____
_____
_____
_____
_____

RESTORING THROUGH APOLOGY

Step 3: Offer Restitution

_____
_____
_____
_____
_____
_____
_____

Step 4: Show Understanding

_____
_____
_____
_____
_____
_____
_____

Step 5: Ask for Forgiveness

_____
_____
_____
_____
_____
_____
_____

A SELF-REFLECTION AND ACTION PLAN

Living blamelessly requires a deeper awareness of how your actions affect others and a commitment to making thoughtful, Christ-centered decisions.

This activity will guide you through reflecting on a single significant action and developing practical strategies, grounded in biblical principles, to minimize the need for forgiveness. By fostering greater self-awareness and intentionality, you can build healthier relationships and reflect Christ's love more fully in every aspect of your life.

Step 1: Self-Reflection on a Signification Action

Choose one significant decision or action you've taken recently. Reflect deeply on this action and answer the following questions:

- How did this action affect others around me?
- Could this action have caused someone to stumble in their faith or been negatively impacted? If so, how?
- What alternative action could I have taken to avoid any negative impact?

_____
_____
_____
_____
_____
_____
_____
_____

A SELF-REFLECTION AND ACTION PLAN

Step 2: Impact Assessment and Action Plan

Identify one key area of your life where this action might have a ripple effect (e.g., family, work, church, social media). For this area:

- What potential stumbling blocks or offenses could this action create
- Develop 2-3 specific strategies you could use to minimize similar risks in the future.
- Choose a Bible verse that can serve as a guide for your behavior in this situation.

A SELF-REFLECTION AND ACTION PLAN

Step 3: Personal Growth and Reflection

Reflect on what you've learned from this process. Are there patterns or habits that this action revealed, and how can you be more mindful in the future?

_____
_____
_____
_____
_____
_____
_____
_____
_____
_____
_____
_____
_____

Step 4: Holding Yourself Accountable

Commit to a weekly self-check-in, reviewing your progress and adjusting your strategies as needed to ensure growth in living blamelessly. Aim to continue this practice for at least one month, using the check-in sheet to hold yourself accountable.

WEEKLY CHECK IN SHEET

Week 1:

Week 2:

Week 3:

Week 4:

Additional Notes:

RESOURCES

Leveraging Our Team

In the journey toward forgiveness and personal growth, collaboration can be a powerful catalyst for transformation. Our team is dedicated to partnering with you, whether you're seeking individual healing or aiming to foster group development.

We offer a range of services, including tailored coaching sessions, immersive workshops, and inspiring keynote presentations, all designed to empower you and your community on the path to forgiveness. With a blend of practical tools, expert guidance, and compassionate support, we create a nurturing environment that encourages meaningful exploration and growth. Together, we can navigate the complexities of grief and forgiveness, unlocking new pathways to healing and wholeness.

PARTNER WITH US: TAILORED PATHS TO FORGIVENESS AND PERSONAL GROWTH

Whether you're seeking individual healing or looking to create a space for group growth, we offer various services designed to guide you along the path of forgiveness. Our approach blends coaching expertise, practical tools, and personalized support, empowering you or your community to move forward with purpose and clarity.

Forgiveness Workshops: Interactive and Transformative Experiences

Our immersive forgiveness workshops are perfect for community groups, churches, corporate teams, and other gatherings looking to explore forgiveness in depth. These workshops include:

- Interactive exercises designed to help participants understand and apply forgiveness concepts.
- Group discussions that encourage shared learning and deeper understanding.
- Actionable tools and personal growth plans to take beyond the workshop.

Each workshop is facilitated with expertise and empathy, creating a safe and supportive space for transformation.

Keynote Speaking: Inspire and Equip Your Audience

As a seasoned public speaker, Katherine Bluma offers powerful, authentic keynote presentations on forgiveness, grief management, and effective communication. Whether addressing church groups, community events, or corporate gatherings, these presentations are designed to inspire and equip attendees with practical steps for their personal growth journey. Each keynote blends personal stories, professional insights, and actionable strategies for living a more fulfilled and forgiving life.

PARTNER WITH US: TAILORED PATHS TO FORGIVENESS AND PERSONAL GROWTH

1:1 Coaching: Personalized Forgiveness Journey

In one-on-one coaching sessions, we provide a tailored approach that focuses specifically on your personal forgiveness journey. As a Master Certified Coach (MCC), we'll work together to address your unique challenges, goals, and pace. This private, confidential setting allows for deep exploration of sensitive topics while developing effective strategies for healing and growth.

Group Coaching: Shared Growth and Collective Healing

Our group coaching sessions foster a supportive, collaborative environment where participants benefit from shared experiences and collective wisdom. Led by a Certified Group Coach (CGC), group sessions are ideal for those who thrive in social learning settings. This option provides both encouragement and accountability, helping everyone on their journey toward forgiveness and healing. Group coaching is also a cost-effective way to access expert guidance and can be customized for various group sizes.

How to Get Started

If you're interested in booking a personal session, organizing a group workshop, or hiring us for an event, we're here to partner with you on your journey to forgiveness. Contact us to explore how we can tailor a coaching or workshop experience that meets your unique needs and creates lasting transformation.

www.ForgivenessFreedomFighter.com/ContactUs